THE MARSHALL LECTURES 1967–68

# MARSHALL, MARX
# AND MODERN TIMES

## THE MULTI-DIMENSIONAL
## SOCIETY

THE MARSHALL LECTURES 1967-68

# MARSHALL, MARX AND MODERN TIMES

## THE MULTI-DIMENSIONAL SOCIETY

BY

## CLARK KERR

*Professor of Economics, University of California*

CAMBRIDGE

AT THE UNIVERSITY PRESS

1969

Published by the Syndics of the Cambridge University Press
Bentley House, 200 Euston Road, London, N.W.1
American Branch: 32 East 57th Street, New York, N.Y. 10022

Library of Congress Catalogue Card Number: 75 92249
S.B.N.: 521 07665 x

Typeset in Great Britain by Alden & Mowbray Ltd, Oxford
and printed in the United States of America

# CONTENTS

*These lectures were delivered at Cambridge in April 1968.*

C.K.

# CHAPTER I

# PRELIMINARY SURVEY

1. It would be a great privilege, under any circumstances, to be invited by the Faculty Board of Economics and Politics to give the Marshall Lectures. It is a very special privilege under the circumstances that surround me, since I have wandered for a decade and a half in the wilderness of academic administration. I like to believe that Professor Marshall would have understood my predicament. He served for four years as Principal of University College of Bristol. At the end of this time (and with the added inspiration of a kidney stone) he sat in the sun in Italy for a year recovering from the experience.

Approaching these lectures I wrote to a friend who had given them on an earlier occasion, asking for the published text. He replied that he had no published text, not because the lectures were out of print, he regretted to say, but because they were never written. He said this was just as well. He came here with detailed notes of a technical nature on a very narrow subject. He said he found himself before what he called a 'heterogeneous' audience. He advised me to make my remarks fit the audience. These lectures are thus intended 'for the general reader'. They deal with the changing institutional context of economic activity rather than with economics proper. This context was of more interest to Marx and also to Marshall than it is to the economist of today.

2. My topic is 'Marshall, Marx and Modern Times'. Marshall is dead. Marx is dead. And the concept of

the working class—with which they were both so concerned—as *the* crucial class in social evolution is dying. But the ideas of Marshall and Marx still influence men and nations; and the visions of manifest destiny perceived for the working class—visions of the day when every worker would be a 'gentleman' or when no man would be in 'chains'—die hard. And few new ideas and few new visions of equal force to those of Marshall and Marx have as yet come along to take their place.

De Tocqueville in *Democracy in America* compared America and Russia. He said the one fought the 'wilderness' with the 'ploughshare'; the other, 'men' with the 'sword'. 'The Anglo-American relies upon personal interest to accomplish his ends...The Russian centres all the authority of society in a single arm...Their starting-point is different, and their courses are not the same; yet each of them seems to be marked out by the will of Heaven to sway the destinies of half the globe.'[1] This was written in 1835. Neither nation does sway half the globe, but the contrasting ideas of 'personal interest' and the 'authority of society' more nearly do; and Marshall came to stand among the greatest exponents of the one idea and Marx of the other.

Marshall was a high priest of the New Economic Liberalism and Marx of the New Political Radicalism. Marshall marked a turning point in liberalism, carrying it beyond natural law and utilitarianism, beyond Smith and Bentham and even John Stuart Mill. Marx marked a turning point in socialism, carrying it beyond the Utopians and the Christian Socialists, beyond Saint-Simon and

[1] Alexis De Tocqueville, *Democracy in America*, London: Oxford University Press, 1961, pp. 286–7.

2

Owen and Kingsley. Both doctrines became more powerful instruments in their hands.

The one doctrine leads men to rely on the free market
and the pricing system, and to doubt the state; the other
emphasizes forced accumulation and growth under the
'social plan' of the state. Both ideas have led to actions with
clear impacts on the past, the present and the future. The
good and the evil of both doctrines live after them. Also
living after them, among other things, is a mutual mis-
trust among the nations that have based their development
on one versus the other of these doctrines.

Marshall and Marx formed their ideas about the
capitalism of roughly a century ago, and much has
happened to capitalism and the world since then. Yet
Schumpeter, who had his doubts about both Marshall and
Marx, could write that Marshall is 'still telling us much it
is worth our while to hear;'[1] and that 'Marx's influence
must be listed among the factors of the scientific situation
today'.[2]

Both Marshall and Marx had world views, nearly all-
embracing systems of thought. They both looked at the
sweep of history and at the breadth of society, and each
discerned an animating principle; and their world views
represent basic historical streams of ideas—the one
emphasizing individual and the other collective action. It
may sound strange to credit Marshall with a world view.
Yet a full reading of him warrants such an attribution, as
against a narrower concentration on his system of short-
run analysis. His broader views are a currently neglected

[1] Joseph A. Schumpeter, 'Alfred Marshall's *Principles*: A Semi-Centennial
Appraisal', *American Economic Review*, June 1941.
[2] Joseph A. Schumpeter, *History of Economic Analysis*, New York: Oxford
University Press, 1954, p. 885.

aspect of Marshall, as, for example, in the new version of the *Encyclopedia of the Social Sciences*. Now I fully realize that the world view has gone out of style in an age of specialization; it is considered primitive in its methods. Division of labour has brought great advances in the realm of analysis as it has in action. But, while we live in an age of specialization, there are some who still look for generalizations—including some of the students of today.

3. How has history dealt with the ideas of Marshall and Marx? I should like to examine this question in the relatively narrow area covered by labour economics; and from the point of view of an American pluralist and pragmatist in the 1960's; and drawing on the historical experience with western, and particularly American, capitalism—which excludes the experience of both western and eastern communism, and of the less industrialized areas of the world. I recognize, of course, that labour economics comprehends only a small part of social evolution; and that America is in some ways unique.

To begin with, it is difficult to speak of the 'ideas' of Marshall and Marx. Each of them wrote a great deal over a prolonged period of time. Marshall's ideas changed somewhat over time. He once spoke of ethics as the 'mistress' and economics as the 'servant'.[1] As Marshall grew older he became more interested in the 'servant' and less in the 'mistress'. Marx switched back and forth all the time between the role of the scientific analyst and that of activist-agitator.

Another handicap is that these two streams of thought have flowed along with only peripheral contact. Joan

[1] Alfred Marshall, Speech at the meeting of the British Economic Association, 19 June 1893, *Economic Journal*, 1893.

Robinson has noted the 'impassable gulf' that long separated the followers of Marx and Marshall: 'The one party was engaged in exploring the evils of the capitalist system, the other in painting it in an agreeable light. One regarded the system as a passing historical phase, containing within itself the germs of its own dissolution; the other regarded the system as a permanent, almost a logical necessity.... This complete difference of attitude made inter-communication between the two schools impossible'[1] and they assaulted each other with 'ill-informed abuse'.[2] As one consequence, there is almost no literature comparing Marshall and Marx, and few economists—the pre-eminent one here at Cambridge—have made major contributions to both schools of thought.

It is not only difficult, but to a degree unfair, to compare Marshall and Marx. Marshall lived from 1842 to 1924; Marx from 1818 to 1883. Thus Marshall had the advantage of an extra generation of historical experience with capitalism. His views were well formulated by the middle 1870's, while Marx had already reached his essential conclusions by the middle 1850's. Marx saw more of the first harsh impact of the factory system, and Marshall more of the 'cheerful stage of capitalism'.[3] Real wages were clearly rising by the time Marshall firmed up his views, although they had fallen at times during the prior century in the England that Marx studied with such detailed interest. Yet the writings of Marx and Engels kept appearing after

[1] Joan Robinson, 'Marx on Unemployment', *Economic Journal*, June–September 1941.

[2] Joan Robinson, *An Essay on Marxian Economics*, London: Macmillan, 1957, p. vi.

[3] Nicholas Kaldor, *Essays on Economic Stability and Growth*, London: Duckworth, 1960, p. 296.

what Marshall saw could be seen by all, and the followers of Marx and Engels had the chance to see even more. But there does remain the contrast of the 1850's and the 1870's.

Yet I should like to look at the ideas of Marx and Marshall together—at their views (1) of the classless society and the perfectibility of man, (2) of the future of capitalism, (3) of class conflict and class collaboration, and (4) of trade unions and group interests. I shall consider the validity of their respective views about their future, which is now our present. From our own perspective, where was each right and where was each wrong? What do their mistakes tell us about the problems of prediction? Finally, I shall try to sketch the nature of the third world of modern times that lies between the free market of Marshall and the 'social plan' of Marx. What is it really like? What are its 'inherent contradictions'? Where may lie the new issues as industrial society further unfolds?

Jacob Viner once said that nothing new could be said about Marshall that was both 'true and significant'.[1] The same might be said about Marx. Yet it may be worthwhile to look at them together and at how the world has evolved in many ways that neither of them foresaw. Such a comparison inevitably takes the form of Marshall versus Marx. Yet, as I shall indicate, Marshall and Marx had more in common than is usually supposed. Among other things, they both looked mainly at Great Britain—the one from a pleasant garden in Cambridge, the other from the gloom of the British Museum. They both wished to save the world and shared the same general goals, differing as to means. The means for one were higher morality and sounder knowledge; for the other, revolution. These

[1] Jacob Viner, *The Long View and the Short*, Glencoe: Free Press, 1958, p. 247.

approaches still divide men. But few men still hold realistically to the goals that Marshall and Marx alike embraced. We are less innocent and less hopeful than either Marshall or Marx. In particular, the transformation of the working class is no longer the key to Utopia as it was for both of them, although it has been an imperative of the industrial system, as I shall later note.

Keynes wrote of Marshall that 'the piercing eyes and ranging wings of an eagle were often called back to earth to do the bidding of the moraliser.'[1] There are those who would say the same of Marx. Such eagles are extinct. But what they saw and hoped to see once stirred the deepest passions of men, and continues to influence our daily lives.

[1] John Maynard Keynes, *Essays in Biography*, New York: Harcourt, Brace, 1933, p. 169.

# CHAPTER 2

# THE CLASSLESS SOCIETY AND THE PERFECTIBILITY OF MAN

1. Marshall and Marx have stood over the decades as opposing prophets representing two contrary views of economic evolution—the one standing for the rightful triumph of capitalism against the challenge of a socialist alternative that would lead to decay; the other for the rightful triumph of communism in the wake of a decaying capitalism. Yet, it is curious how much they thought alike; how much they stood together in their views of the world; how much they both differed together from more contemporary views. Their areas of agreement are as interesting as their areas of disagreement, and are helpful to an understanding of their disagreements.

Marshall has been thought of as the economist of the middle class, but his concern lay rather with the workers and with poverty. He once wrote 'I have devoted myself ... to the problem of poverty, and ... very little of my work has been devoted to any inquiry which does not bear on that'.[1] Pigou tells of how Marshall bought a small oil painting of a man 'down and out' and called it his 'patron saint'[2]—a painting that now hangs in the Marshall Library. Some of Marshall's earliest writing was for a labour paper called the *Bee-Hive*[3]; his earliest teaching

[1] *Official Papers of Alfred Marshall*, London: Macmillan, 1926, p. 205.

[2] A. C. Pigou, *Alfred Marshall and Current Thought*, London: Macmillan, 1953, pp. 64–5.

[3] R. Harrison (Ed.), 'Two Early Articles by Alfred Marshall', *Economic Journal*, September 1963.

8

included workers' education classes; and his early friends numbered leaders of the trade union movement. In his *Economics of Industry* he listed among the 'urgent social problems' that constituted the 'aims' of the economist the following questions:[1] 'Is it necessary that large numbers of the people should be exclusively occupied with work that has no elevating character?' and 'Is it possible to educate gradually among the great mass of workers a new capacity for the higher kinds of work; and in particular for under-taking co-operatively the management of the businesses in which they are themselves employed?' Marshall served as president of the Cooperative Congress. He was one of the earliest economists of note to have intimate knowledge of trade union operations. Keynes considered his analysis of trade unions to be 'the first satisfactory treatment on modern lines' of this important topic,[2] and said that Marshall sympathized with the labour movement and also with socialism 'in every way except intellectually'[3]—but I believe there was a degree of intellectual sympathy as well.

Marshall spoke in the *Principles*, in what now sounds like a very condescending manner, of the need of econo-mists to have what he called 'class sympathy'[4]—meaning sympathy for the labouring classes; but this is not the tone of his famous essay on 'The Future of the Working Classes'[5] which is more of empathy than of condescension.

[1] Alfred Marshall, *Economics of Industry*, London: Macmillan, 1928, pp. 30 and 31.

[2] Keynes, *Essays in Biography*, p. 217.

[3] *Ibid.*, p. 238.

[4] Alfred Marshall, *Principles*, London: Macmillan, 1920, p. 45.

[5] 'The Future of the Working Classes' in A. C. Pigou (ed.), *Memorials of Alfred Marshall*, New York: Kelley and Millman, 1956.

Whether condescension or empathy, it was to the working class, not the middle class, that Marshall gave his attention and his concern.

For Marx, the working class was not only at the centre of his concern as the exploited element of capitalist society, but it also held within itself—far more than for Marshall— the determination of the future. The inevitable evolution of the working class was the engine of social change.

2. The welfare of the working class was central for both Marshall and Marx, and this welfare called for the disappearance of the class itself. The goal for Marshall was the 'abolition of all classes', including the working class, in the classless society, and he expressed this goal in a particularly Victorian fashion. 'Progress' was to continue 'till the official distinction between working man and gentleman has passed away', 'till...every man is a gentleman'; and he said that 'I hold that it may and that it will' happen. This was in 1873. By 1923, he added the note that this view 'bears marks of the over-sanguine temperament of youth', but he did not retract it.[1] In 1919, in his *Industry and Trade*, he was still writing of 'the decline of exclusive class advantages in industry'.[2] Every man was to become a 'gentleman' through 'better education', less 'excessive strain on muscles', 'shortened hours', greater wealth more equally shared. When all this had transpired, 'in so far as the working classes are men who have such excessive work to do, in so far will the working classes have been

[1] 'The Future of the Working Classes' in A. C. Pigou (ed.), *Memorials of Alfred Marshall*, New York: Kelley and Millman, 1956.
[2] Alfred Marshall, *Industry and Trade*, London: Macmillan, 1919, Book III, Chapter 14.

abolished'.[1] The classless society for Marshall was one in which all men were 'civilised'[2]—were gentlemen.

To Marx, the classless society was one where exploitation and the domination of one man over another no longer existed—it was the heavy hand of the capitalist more than heavy work on the job that had to go. But for both Marshall and Marx the expectation was a society with social equality. They both subscribed to the goal of 'from each according to his ability, to each according to his need' and Marshall said that in this 'one sense indeed I am a socialist'.[3]

3. Both were optimists not only about the first coming of the classless society but also about the perfectibility of human nature in that better society—for Marshall, an improvement in human nature was both cause and effect of an improved social order; for Marx, it was effect only and not cause. But human nature for both was clearly malleable and in a favourable direction. For Marx, 'socialism will transform society; and human nature with it'.[4] This was a major tenet of his faith.

The Marshallian view was more complex—morality led to material welfare which led to higher morality in a never-ending upward spiral. It started, not with the revolution, but with the mothers: 'The character of the nation depends chiefly on that of the mothers of the nation—on their firmness and gentleness and sincerity. It is in childhood and at home, that the workman must

[1] Pigou (ed.), 'The Future of the Working Classes'.

[2] T. H. Marshall, *Citizenship and Social Class*, Cambridge: University Press, 1950, p. 7.

[3] Alfred Marshall in *Industrial Remuneration Conference*, London: Cassell, 1885, p. 173.

[4] M. M. Bober, *Karl Marx's Interpretation of History*, Cambridge: Harvard University Press, 1950, p. 81.

learn to be truthful and trusty, cleanly and careful, energetic and thorough, to reverence others and to respect himself.'[1] 'Moral character' is a firm basis for the 'growth of wealth'.[2] 'Material' welfare then, in turn, raises 'spiritual' welfare.[3] 'Human will, guided by careful thought, can so modify circumstances as largely to modify character.'[4] With character encouraging wealth and wealth encouraging character, 'The average level of human nature in the Western world has risen rapidly during the last 50 years'; 'the working classes have become better educated, less addicted to coarse enjoyments, and more appreciative of the quiet of a many roomed house with a garden'; and even 'the number of intelligent and upright directors increases'.[5] All was for the better in an ever better world. Here again Marshall compared himself to the socialists. He spoke in his Inaugural Lecture at Cambridge of his sympathy for socialist views on the 'perfectibility of man'.[6] But he saw no sudden improvement, after any kind of a revolution, for, as he later wrote, 'human nature improves slowly'.[7] For Marx, men could be catapulted into a better world; for Marshall, there were no great leaps forward.

Jacob Viner wrote that Marshall 'had faith in the

[1] Alfred Marshall and Mary Paley Marshall, *The Economics of Industry* London: Macmillan, 1881, p. 12. (This is to be distinguished from *Economics of Industry* by Alfred Marshall alone.) Marshall 'came to regard this little book with disfavour' (see C. W. Guillebaud in Volume II of the Variorum edition of the *Principles*, London: Macmillan, 1961, p. 12).

[2] *Ibid.*

[3] Pigou, 'The Future of the Working Classes'. *op. cit.*

[4] A. Marshall, *Principles*, p. 48.

[5] All quoted from T. W. Hutchison, *A Review of Economic Doctrines*, Oxford: Clarendon Press, 1962, p. 93.

[6] Alfred Marshall, *The Present Position of Economics*, London: Macmillan, 1885, p. 17.

[7] A. Marshall, *Economics of Industry*, p. 413.

effectiveness of sound moral preaching to produce the goodwill and of sound Cambridge economics to produce the understanding'[1] that would lead to a better world. The burden placed on Cambridge was indeed great. Marshall hoped 'to increase the numbers of those, whom Cambridge, the great mother of strong men, sends out into the world with cool heads but warm hearts, willing to give some at least of their best powers to grappling with the social suffering around them'.[2] To Marx, it was not the Cambridge economists but Communist Party comrades who would really save the world; and the rallying cry was 'workers of the world unite', not 'sound Cambridge economics'. But the world would be saved, one way or the other.

Marshall thought 'we are not in a position to guess confidently to what goal the advance thus begun will ultimately lead'[3]—but advance there was. Advance there was also in prospect for Marx and he was fully confident. Marshall had a certainty about what was right and a hope about what would come to be; Marx had a certainty both about what was wrong and how it would be righted.

4. Some of the central forces at work on society were seen in much the same way by both men. Technology was basic. 'In acquiring new productive forces', said Marx, 'men change their mode of production.... The windmill gives you society with the feudal lord; the steam-mill society with the industrial capitalist.'[4] Marshall, while less historically oriented, took the importance of technology

---

[1] Viner, *The Long View and the Short*, p. 251.

[2] A. Marshall, *The Present Position of Economics*, p. 57.

[3] A. Marshall, *Principles*, p. 46.

[4] Karl Marx, *The Poverty of Philosophy*, London: Martin Lawrence, 1884, p. 119.

for granted. He knew that the technology and the skill that went with it affected wages. 'He could tell before-hand,' by watching the work process, 'what wages were being paid for any kind of work and was seldom wrong by more than a few pence a week';[1] and he believed that 'in the modern world the chief readjustments of the remuneration of labour are associated with changes in process'.[2]

The entrepreneur played a crucial role as the accumulator of power and surplus value for Marx; and as the source of initiative and progress for Marshall. So also, both saw a central role for profits—it was the incentive that kept the system moving and the source of funds for its movement. For both men, additionally, the economic role was the dominant one in the lives of men. To Marx, men reflected their class; and the relations of production were the basic forces overwhelming all others. Marshall was less global—work, not class, determined behaviour. He could say that 'man's character' is 'formed by his daily work', that 'poverty causes degradation', and that 'bodily and mental health and strength are much influenced by occupation'.[3] Class position for the one and job specifications for the other were basic to personal conduct.

Thus for both, technology, the entrepreneur, profits, and occupational role were key ingredients to under-standing the social process.

They also thought they saw some of the same things happening to society—the concentration of economic

[1] Mary Paley Marshall, *What I Remember*, Cambridge: University Press, 1947, p. 43.

[2] Alfred Marshall, *Money, Credit and Commerce*, New York: Augustus Kelley, 1960, p. 239.

[3] A. Marshall, *Principles*, pp. 1, 2, and 198.

effort through the growth of large-scale enterprises, a declining rate of profit, a decline in labour's relative share of income as the profit share grew, and the development of a 'Residuum' (Marshall) of the unemployable or near unemployable or a 'lumpen proletariat' (Marx) thrown off by advancing capitalism—a group arising below the working class.

Alike they distrusted the state under capitalism— Marshall because it was inefficient and a potential drag on progress; Marx because it was the tool of the bourgeoisie to keep its supremacy, the 'instrument of class rule'.[1] Under a fully developed communism, for Marx, the state was to 'wither' away. Marshall distrusted the state but, it should be noted, saw a greater place for it than did many of his contemporaries. Beyond providing for external security and domestic law and order, he saw it playing a positive role in advancing education, encouraging trade unions, reducing the inequality of incomes, providing for public health and city planning, preventing restrictive combinations, giving relief to the poor through constructive work. The state should not operate economic enterprises, but it could increase welfare in many ways. It took Keynes, however, to make the role of the state in guiding economic affairs more respectable under capitalism, and Lenin to make it more forceful in fact under communism than it ever had been under capitalism. The followers of both Marshall and Marx saw more of a role for the state than did their mentors.

Marx and Marshall both stressed the importance of the British to world history and saw them behaving in much

---

[1] Paul Sweezy, *The Theory of Capitalist Development*, Oxford University Press, 1942, p. 349.

the same way—one regretting the behaviour and the other lauding it. To Marx, the recalcitrant 'English possess all material requisites of the social revolution. But they lack the spirit of generalisation and revolutionary passion'.[1] To Marshall, the moral 'Anglo-Saxons have generally eschewed the more anti-social forms both of competition and combination'.[2]

Finally, they both had what Homan once called Marshall's 'messianic quality'.[3]

Marshall and Marx had more in common, in these several ways, than their popular locations at opposite poles imply. Marshall was more sympathetic to aspects of socialism and Marx more of a Victorian utopian than the surviving image of either allows—Shove once referred to Marx as 'that other eminent Victorian'.[4] They both assumed that man is inherently good; that economic environments, historically more or less evil, could be greatly improved; that improved economic environments would lead to a better society all around and to better men.

5. So much of what they held together, as fellow members of the Victorian Age, divides them from more current views. The working class, as a separate class with its own 'consciousness', today is often seen more as representing the past than the future. Clear class distinctions have largely disappeared but infinitely graded status differentials still stand in the way of the classless society.

[1] Max Beer (ed.), 'Selections from the Literary Revisions of Karl Marx', *The Labour Monthly*, July 1923.

[2] A. Marshall, *Industry and Trade*, p. 652.

[3] Paul Homan, *Contemporary Economic Thought*, New York: Harper & Brothers, 1928, p. 9.

[4] G. F. Shove, 'Place of Marshall's *Principles* in the Development of Economic Theory', *Economic Journal*, December 1942.

Optimism about the perfectibility of human nature has given way at best to scepticism; and more of the problems of man are now seen to be inherent directly in man himself and not the sole fault of any particular economic or social system.

It is also clear by now that personal points of view reflect more than just class position or occupational role; that ideas also contend for influence as against the economic base for opinions. The state under capitalism is now more often seen less as impediment or oppressor and more as a progressive force and a source of security. The messianic urge has often given way to the prophecy of doom. Dystopias have replaced Utopias. There are few visions any more of every man a gentleman and each in his own version of Marshall's Baliol Croft in a Cambridge garden. The vision is more likely to be *1984.*

The radicals and liberals of today are divided by the degree of their pessimism, not the certainty of their optimism about a better world—both men and their economic environments are always more or less evil; and neither the radical nor the liberal any longer assumes that an improvement in economic conditions necessarily guarantees an improvement in society as a whole—in fact, other aspects of society may deteriorate. When the trouble with the world was a society that could be changed, there was naturally more cause for optimism than today when the trouble appears to be also with man himself who is less subject to change. Utopia no longer appears so likely so soon—if ever; and its foundations—if any—lie not in the economy alone.

Marshall and Marx belong to another age. What united them in their hopes for the classless society and the perfectibility of man separates them from the contemporary world. Yet what separated them as to the means to be followed still unites the major forces and ideologies that oppose each other in the world of today. We turn now to a consideration of the points of disagreement.

# CHAPTER 3

# THE FUTURE OF CAPITALISM

1. What separated Marshall and Marx was disagreement about the future of capitalism.

Marshall was generally optimistic and Marx generally pessimistic; but Marshall had his reservations. He warned that British capitalism faced 'stiffness of joints that is almost inevitable in each old industry, and in the general relations of industries and trades in each old country'.[1] He hoped that 'the short-sighted selfishness which has developed the evil practice of stinting output (whether by trade unions or by employers' associations on the cartel model)' might 'be abandoned' and thus Britain 'may prosper; but she may rapidly fall from her high place, if she becomes slack in any respect'.[2] He feared that scientific, technological and managerial leadership was passing to Germany and America.

Marx was certain that capitalism would disappear. The question was whether it would always go out with a bang or occasionally with a whimper: 'We do not deny that there are countries, like England and America and ... I might add Holland, where the worker may attain his object by peaceful means';[3] but this was seen as the exception.

'Stiffness' intruded on Marshall's guarded optimism, and the possibility of a peaceful evolution tempered Marx's

[1] A. Marshall, *Industry and Trade*, p. 103.

[2] *Ibid.*, p. 655.

[3] Karl Kautsky, *The Labour Revolution*, London: Allen and Unwin, 1925, p. 24.

assurance about the revolution. As it turned out, the intruding doubts of both have held a better key to some of subsequent history than the more general views of each on the viability of capitalism. Their occasional fears were more realistic than their general hopes, particularly in relation to England.

2. For Marx, the general view was that capitalism was so rife with contradictions that it must fall: 'The bourgeoisie ... produces ... its own grave-diggers.'[1] The main culprit was the falling rate of profit. Workers were replaced by new technology but the displacement of labour was greater than its reabsorption[2] because the decline in the rate of profit did not provide the basis for full re-employment. Additionally, partly because of the falling rate of profit, there was cyclical instability which gave rise to crises of overproduction. The cycles of accumulation became ever more severe. To general unemployment were added ever deepening depressions. In the end, the system collapsed.

Marshall, on the contrary, saw no tendency for increasing unemployment and more severe depressions. He regretted unemployment: 'Forced interruption to labour is a terrible evil';[3] but he had faith that it was temporary, that equilibrium would be more or less automatically restored at full employment levels, although he considered the downward stickiness of money wages under

[1] Karl Marx and Frederick Engels, *Manifesto of the Communist Party*, Chicago: Charles H. Kerr, 1913, p. 29.

[2] Fred M. Gottheil, *Marx's Economic Predictions*, Evanston: Northwestern University Press, 1966, p. 203. Marx assumed that new technology was heavily labour-saving. (W. Fellner, 'Marxian Hypotheses and Observable Trends Under Capitalism: A "Modernised" Interpretation', *Economic Journal*, March 1957.)

[3] A. Marshall, *Industrial Remuneration Conference*, p. 175.

trade unionism as an impediment to this self-adjusting process. He largely neglected the business cycle and unemployment—they were passing misfortunes, not the death knell of the system. 'An advance of technique is frequently accompanied by temporary dislocations of employment', but 'its benefits are likely to be many times as great as the harm which it works.'[1]

3. Employment, to Marx, was almost as undesirable as unemployment. His views of the machine under capitalism were those of a 'machine-breaker': 'Owing to the extensive use of machinery and to division of labour, the work of the proletarians has lost all individual character, and, consequently, all charm for the workman. He becomes an appendage of the machine, and it is only the most simple, most monotonous, and most easily acquired knack that is required of him.'[2] In his discussion of 'the strife between workmen and machine',[3] Marx tells how the machine takes away the workers' skill and even his job, and breaks his strikes. Women and children take the place of men; the working day is lengthened; the pace of work is intensified.[4] The evils of the machine in the factory are all-pervasive. It 'exhausts the nervous system', 'confiscates every atom of freedom', and 'deprives the work of all interest'.[5] All in all, there is 'the transformation of the labourers into labouring cattle' in a system 'utterly prodigal with human life'.[6] Employed workers had

[1] A. Marshall, *Money, Credit and Commerce*, p. 244.

[2] Marx and Engels, *Manifesto of the Communist Party*, p. 21.

[3] Karl Marx, *Capital, Volume One* (edited by Frederick Engels), Chicago: Charles H. Kerr, 1909, p. 466.

[4] *Ibid.*, p. 430 ff.

[5] Quoted from Bober, *Karl Marx's Interpretation of History*, pp. 211 and 212.

[6] Karl Marx, *Capital, Volume Three* (edited by Frederick Engels), Chicago: Charles H. Kerr, 1909, p. 104.

almost as much cause to revolt as the unemployed; the living employed could almost envy the dying unemployed.

Marx saw a great 'depreciation of the human world'[1] — psychic as well as economic deprivation. The worker was alienated from his product by the surplus value that went to the capitalist; from his work by the machine; from himself and from other men as everything got turned into money through cash transactions. Alienation of the employed was seen as a constant companion to unemployment on the high road to revolution.

The machine and division of labour were evil under capitalism. In some unexplained fashion, communist society would do away with division of labour. Marx sounded like a modern-day Maoist, for communism 'makes it possible for me to do one thing today and another tomorrow, to hunt in the morning, fish in the afternoon, rear cattle in the evening, criticize after dinner, just as I have a mind, without ever becoming a hunter, fisherman, shepherd or critic'.[2] There were to be no specialists and no experts in the communist world of the future. The wage system was to be abolished. External discipline over workers would become unnecessary, since each would come to discipline himself. And, 'in a communistic society, there would be a very different scope for employment of machinery than there can be in a bourgeois society'.[3] The machine is one thing under capitalism, and apparently would be quite another under communism. The metal leopard would lose its spots.

[1] Herbert Marcuse, *Reason and Revolution*, New York: Humanities Press, 1963, p. 274.

[2] Karl Marx and Frederick Engels, *German Ideology*, New York: International Publishers, 1939, p. 22.

[3] Marx, *Capital, Volume One*, p. 429n.

# The Future of Capitalism

To Marshall, on the other hand, the machine *per se* was mostly good, and so also was the division of labour that went with it. 'Complex machinery increases the demand for judgment and general intelligence.' 'Machinery relieves the strain on human muscles.' 'Machinery takes over sooner or later all monotonous work in manufacture.'[1] The machine elevated man, and division of labour was fundamental to economic progress. It was the machine—not man—that should work the long hours and 'men in alternate shifts should work short hours. In this movement I see a great hope for the improvement of the human race'.[2] The machine brought improvement, not alienation.

Jobs, to Marshall, became more skilled and more responsible. In the *Principles*, he wrote of rising skill levels[3] and once estimated that the ratio of skilled to unskilled jobs had doubled in the quarter century after 1850; and this did not fully take into account the fact that jobs that still carried the same names changed greatly in their content[4]—they looked the same but had become different and in a favourable direction. Even if real wages for the same jobs remained the same (and they did not), the working classes had benefitted because a higher proportion had moved into skilled grades.[5]

To Marx, it was the other way around. 'The centralization of capital involves a greater division of labour and a greater use of machinery. The greater division of labour destroys the especial skill of the labourer; and by putting

---

[1] A. Marshall, *Principles*, pp. 257, 261, 262.
[2] Alfred Marshall, Letter to *The Times*, January 18, 1887.
[3] *Op. cit.*, p. 716.
[4] *Official Papers*, pp. 95 and 96.
[5] A. Marshall, *Industrial Remuneration Conference*, p. 187.

## The Future of Capitalism

in the place of this skilled work labour which any one can perform, it increases competition among workers…and the reward of labour diminishes for all, and the burden of labour increases for some.'[1] Jobs deteriorated in their content, rather then being improved.

4. Marshall saw the standard of living rising steadily. Both he and Marx repudiated the 'wages fund' doctrine. To Marshall, wages were 'a flow of income to be distributed',[2] not a fixed fund; and population was subject to control, particularly within the middle class. Real wages rose with the 'efficiency of work' and there were many causes of greater efficiency. Higher real wages were even self-generating; the higher they went, the higher they would go: 'We conclude then that an increase of wages, unless earned under unwholesome conditions, almost always increases the strength, physical, mental and even moral, of the coming generation; and that, other things being equal, an increase in the earnings that are to be got by labour increases its rate of growth.'[3] Sources of higher real wages were better technique, additional capital, better education which increased 'those who are capable of the more difficult work of the world' and diminished 'the number of those who can do only unintelligent work'.[4] Shorter hours could also 'increase efficiency in several ways, among others by enabling the worker to hold himself better in hand, and therefore to manage more delicate and complex machinery'.[5] Nor did the single trade that gained efficiency alone benefit since 'increased efficiency

---

[1] Marx, *The Poverty of Philosophy*, pp. 101–102.
[2] Alfred Marshall, 'Wages and Profits', *Quarterly Journal of Economics*, 1888.
[3] A. Marshall, *Principles*, p. 532.
[4] A. Marshall, *Industrial Remuneration Conference*, p. 182.
[5] A. Marshall, Letter to *The Times*.

in any trade tends to raise real wages in others'.[1] All taken together, 'progress is fast improving the condition of the great body of the working classes'.[2]

Marshall saw real wages rising even though labour's share was falling. He relied on some early work of Bowley for the idea that 'the increase of wages' has been 'a little less, proportionately, than the increase of income in general'.[3] This was in error, but he made the best of it by arguing that the capital share must rise so that real wages could rise since capital accumulation is basic to higher real wages. He did not fully realize that the capital share might fall and real wages still rise through a lower price for capital, improved technology embodied in capital, and increased skill associated with the use of capital.[4] But he did show, which is true, that the class share and real wages do not necessarily move in the same direction.

Improving conditions in the Marshallian view are replaced by 'increasing misery' in the Marxian. It was clear to Marx that there was 'increasing misery' but it is not clear *in* Marx what 'increasing misery' really meant. Certainly he meant that labour's percentage share of total income declined as capital accumulation grew. At times he seemed to say also that the worker's real wage declined—that the 'poor became poorer'; at others that it rose absolutely but declined relatively as a 'house' became a 'hut' when a 'palace' went up next door—it was the 'social gulf' that widened; and at still others that the real

[1] A. Marshall, *Principles*, 539.

[2] *Ibid.*, p. 687.

[3] Alfred Marshall, 'Discussion on Mr. Bowley's "Changes in Average Wages" ,' *Journal of the Statistical Society*, 1895.

[4] S. G. Checkland, 'Marshall and the Wages-Wealth Paradox', *Economic Journal*, June 1957.

problem of 'increasing misery' was in the non-economic aspects of life as the worker was turned into a 'fragment of a man', became subject to the 'slavery' of capitalist domination. When reading about 'increasing misery', one can be sympathetic with the comment of Pareto that the ideas of Marx were like bats—you could never be sure whether you were seeing a mouse or a bird.[1]

A reasonable reading of Marx, it seems to me, is that almost anything could happen to real wages, particularly in the short-run, and thus to 'misery', but that one particular outcome was more likely than any other. He held to a bargaining theory of wages, that wages would be set between the minimum at which the worker could exist and the maximum the employer could pay and still remain in business. 'Between the two limits...an immense scale of variations is possible;' and the result depends on the 'respective powers of the combatants'.[2] Thus Engels could write to Bebel that 'Marx has proved...that the laws regulating wages...are in no sense iron but on the contrary very elastic'.[3]

Marx saw wages as elastic, but mostly in a downward direction. The tendency was to push wages to the 'minimum limit'.[4] This minimum limit might be 'the lowest and the only necessary rate of wages...which provides for the subsistence of the worker during work and for a supplement adequate to raise a family so that the race of workers does not die out',[5] or it might be 'determined

---

[1] See reference in Bober, *Karl Marx's Interpretation of History*, p. 297.

[2] Karl Marx, *Value, Price and Profit*, London: Allen and Unwin, 1925, p. 88.

[3] Karl Marx and Frederick Engels, *Selected Correspondence*, New York: International Publishers, 1942, Letter 161, p. 335.

[4] Marx, *Value, Price and Profit*, p. 92.

[5] Karl Marx, *Early Writings*, London: Watts and Company, 1963, p. 69.

by a traditional standard of life' which was not 'mere physical life'.[1] Whatever the minimum, 'wages are determined by the bitter struggle between capitalist and worker' that results in 'the necessary victory of the capitalist'.[2] The capitalist has more holding power; it is easier for him to combine; and, particularly, he has on his side the 'reserve army of the unemployed' ever augmented by population increase, technological displacement, depressions, the concentration of effort into ever fewer firms, the addition of women and children to the labour force. The 'relative surplus-population is therefore the pivot upon which the law of demand and supply of labour works. It confines the field of action of this law within the limits absolutely convenient to the activity of exploitation and to the domination of capital'.[3] 'Thus the minimum of wages is the natural price of labour', and this minimum was only sufficient for the worker 'to sustain himself, however badly, and of propagating his race, however slightly'. He may even receive 'below the minimum in times of industrial stagnation'.[4] Misery increased more at some times than at others; but misery there always was—it accumulated along with capital.

It is possible in the light of history to put a favourable interpretation on the 'misery' of Marx by referring to a falling share of wages and a rising level of subsistence.[5] But the important facts are not the fall in the relative share—rather, the absolute constancy of that share; not

[1] Marx, *Value, Price and Profit*, p. 86.

[2] Marx, *Early Writings*, p. 69.

[3] Marx, *Capital, Volume One*, p. 701.

[4] Marx, *The Poverty of Philosophy*, p. 205.

[5] Thomas Sowell, 'Marx's "Increasing Misery" Doctrine', *American Economic Review*, March 1960.

a rising level of subsistence—rather, the rising level of affluence. Yet it is rather harsh to dismiss Marx, as Samuelson did in reviewing these controversies, as 'a minor post-Ricardian'.[1]

5. Marx saw injustice all around him under capitalism; Marshall, a kind of rough justice. In Marshall, the worker received the 'net value' of his labour and the capitalist a profit rate that 'diminishes slowly from generation to generation',[2] and this seemed reasonably just, since 'an absolutely fair rate of remuneration belongs to Utopia'.[3] In any event, 'the main benefits...accrue to the consumers: that is, to the working classes'.[4] There is little exploitation and less and less misery. Sacrifices and rewards are roughly balanced. The good economic order and the good political order, moreover, went hand in hand, for a free economic system encouraged a free political system. 'Economic Liberalism according to the Marshallian view, is the theory that Capitalism—itself a changing, evolving structure—offers greater promise for economic welfare than any other system about which we have knowledge at the present stage of social evolution.'[5] Marshall saw a sunny world of economic and political freedom that held promise. He saw 'competitive capitalism...at the zenith of its achievement' after 'a long vista of comparative stagnation'.[6]

6. Another major difference between Marx and Marshall

[1] Paul A. Samuelson, 'Wages and Interest: A Modern Dissection of Marxian Economic Models', *American Economic Review*, December 1957.

[2] A. Marshall, *Industry and Trade*, p. 72.

[3] 'A Fair Rate of Wages' in Pigou (ed.), *Memorials of Alfred Marshall*.

[4] A. Marshall, *Industry and Trade*, p. 72.

[5] M. S. Heath, 'Variorum Edition of Marshall's *Principles*', *Southern Economic Journal*, July 1963.

[6] Shove, 'Place of Marshall's *Principles*'.

was in their views of education. Marx was little concerned with it. He saw it mainly in the service of the capitalist, providing the technical, vocational and professional training that the capitalists needed;[1] and 'labour is only a commodity like others'.[2] Marx said that to make capital rich, 'each labourer must be made poor in individual productive powers'.[3] He spoke of the school system as devised to assure 'intellectual desolation' which was worse than 'natural ignorance';[4] aside from 'some little instruction in technology and in the practical handling of the various implements of labour'.[5]

Marshall, on the other hand, saw great values in education and particularly for the individual, and the individual worker was not viewed as a commodity. He spoke of 'education' as 'a national investment'.[6] 'Much of the best natural ability in the nation is born among the working classes, and too often runs to waste now'[7]—and education could help correct that, although he saw the difficulty in moving from one class status to another. He thought that the 'most valuable of all capital is that invested in human beings'.[8] Commodities could not improve themselves; human beings could. Marshall recognized the difficulties inherent in this form of investment, then made mostly by parents who varied greatly in their ability and willingness to undertake the invest-

[1] See Marx, *Capital, Volume One*, p. 534.

[2] See Marx, *Value, Price and Profit*, p. 83.

[3] Marx, *Capital, Volume One*, p. 397.

[4] *Ibid.*, p. 436.

[5] *Ibid.*, p. 534.

[6] A. Marshall, *Principles*, p. 216. (Professor Theodore Schultz of the University of Chicago has particularly renewed and strengthened the idea of 'investment in man'. See *The Economic Value of Education*, New York: Columbia, 1963.)

[7] *Ibid.*, p. 212.

[8] *Ibid.*, p. 564.

## The Future of Capitalism

ment; and 'those who bear the expenses of rearing and educating (the worker) receive but very little of the price that is paid for his services in later years'.[1] Yet he favoured workers investing their higher wages in the 'Personal Capital of themselves and their children' so that the effects could be 'cumulative' from 'generation to generation'.[2] 'And the economic value of one great industrial genius is sufficient to cover the expenses of the education of a whole town.'[3] He also favoured more education for executives—which was a far advanced view for his time—and hoped that 'more University men' might prepare for the 'higher posts of business'.[4] This view of a growing accumulation of 'human capital' redounding to the credit of the individual and of society is one of the principle sources of the optimism of Marshall as against the pessimism of Marx. Increasing education took the place of 'increasing misery'.

7. Where Marshall saw considerable freedom and a rough approximation of justice, Marx saw domination and exploitation—economic and political. Where Marshall saw promise, Marx saw decay. Where Marshall saw equilibrium, Marx saw disequilibrium. How do their views on the future of capitalism look, now that what was to them the future has passed partially into history?

Capitalism has developed some 'stiffness' in some places, as Marshall feared, but stiffness since World War II has become such a departure from the common rule that it

[1] A. Marshall, *Principles*, 560–1.(Professor Theodore Schultz of the University of Chicago has particularly renewed and strengthened the idea of 'investment in man'. See *The Economic Value of Education*, New York: Columbia, 1963.)

[2] A. Marshall, *Economics of Industry*, p. 391.

[3] A. Marshall, *Principles*, p. 216.

[4] A. Marshall, *The Present Position of Economics*, p. 55.

constitutes a national crisis where it does appear. Generally growth has been at an accelerating rate, but the final verdict of history has not been passed. With growth has gone reasonably peaceful evolution; and what was the exception for Marx has been the universal experience— nowhere has an advanced capitalist nation been subject to violent and permanent revolutionary change internally generated by the increasing contradictions of its society.

Marx was right about the growing seriousness of depressions, but he did not see that they could eventually be brought under control; but then Marshall hardly saw them at all. The machine has been accepted and even increasingly welcomed and certainly has improved the overall lot of the worker, as Marshall saw so well; and it has been communism that has particularly sought to enthrone the machine that Marx so detested under capitalism and—in its Russian but not yet its Chinese form—that has so sung the praises of the resulting specialization. Alienation there certainly is, but it now seems to adhere to large-scale industrial societies, under whatever auspices, not capitalism alone; and to adhere also to individuals in the family and in the community, not just in the factory.

Some things have clearly improved. Jobs stand at a higher level of skill. Labour's relative share has remained constant or even risen. Real wages of employed workers rise steadily. Education does add to human capital. 'Justice', however, is no longer defined so simply as either the net value product or the full product of labour; it has come to mean mostly just 'more'.

Overall, Marshall saw the future of capitalism (with the very major exception of his lack of concern for depressions) more clearly than did Marx. The paradox is, however, that so much of the world came to follow Marx, not Marshall, in the intervening period. There is an adequate explanation for this paradox, as I shall note later.

From current perspective, the economic system—whether capitalist or socialist—is less the source either of all good or all evil than either Marshall or Marx believed. There is more to good and evil than was comprehended by either philosophy. What Marx saw wrong with capitalism (exploitation) and Marshall with socialism (lack of full freedom of choice and of initiative) are wrong with the industrial world.

# CHAPTER 4

# CLASS CONFLICT AND
# CLASS COLLABORATION

1. Class to Marshall was not a central concern. He spoke feelingly about the working class, as we have seen, and admired the virtues of the middle class—particularly its propensity to marry late—but the idea of a class structure was rather foreign to his way of thinking. He thought more in terms of functions performed than in terms of class position. However, he did have class categories in which people could be placed, and he had views about the morality and the evolution of each class. While he never set forth a precise class structure, it is possible to identify six not wholly distinct classes: the entrepreneurs, the middle class of the professional personnel, the 'intermediate class' of the 'highly skilled, highly paid artisan',[1] the working class of manual labourers, the rentier class, and the 'Residuum' of the unemployable and near unemployable.

The first four classes were all productive. He had little use for the last two and rather wished they would go away. The 'Residuum', in fact, was to be 'attacked in its strongholds'.[2] He saw the rentier class and the 'Residuum' hopefully disappearing, and he saw the working class and the intermediate class merging into the middle class, which would also embrace the entrepreneurs. Economic progress, education and morality brought this gradually

[1] Pigou (ed.), *Memorials of Alfred Marshall*, pp. 104–105.
[2] *Ibid.*, p. 387.

about. He particularly thought that 'the mutual dependence' of capital and labour is the 'closest';[1] that they pros-
pered together. There was one fly in the ointment.
Contrary to economic reality, in Britain, most regretfully,
'class consciousness is cherished by the manual worker
with an almost religious fervour'.[2] Marshall favoured,
instead, class collaboration.

Collaboration with the class enemy was a clear evil to
Marx. The theory of social classes was central to the
thought of Marx, but nowhere did he give it a sustained
treatment. The last chapter of the last volume of *Capital*
was headed 'The Classes', but it constituted a few notes
only and not a theory. Yet, as Schumpeter states, Marx was
the first to have a theory of social classes.[3] Classes, Marx
believed, followed the roles played by people in production and it is customary to say that he had two classes:
capital and labour. Actually his system was more
complex.

In his unfinished chapter on 'The Classes', Marx noted
three classes: wage labourers, capitalists and landlords. He
also saw 'middle and transition stages'[4] and he wrote at
times of the self-employed who owned their own capital
and captured their own surplus value, and of service
workers, like doctors, who in effect sold their own time
and skill.[5] Beyond that, he talked of the 'lumpen-
proletariat'—'the social scum, that passively rotting mass
thrown off by the lowest layers of the old society'[6]. Thus

[1] A. Marshall, *Principles*, p. 544.
[2] A. Marshall, *Industry and Trade*, p. 391.
[3] Schumpeter, *A History of Economic Analysis*, p. 552.
[4] Marx, *Capital, Volume Three*, p. 1031.
[5] Karl Marx, *Theories of Surplus Value* (edited by Karl Kautsky), London: Lawrence and Wishert, 1951, pp. 192–7.
[6] Marx and Engels, *Manifesto of the Communist Party*, p. 27.

it may be said that he had a five-class structure: the capitalists, the landlords, the workers, a 'transition class', and the lumpen-proletariat.

The bourgeoisie had once been useful when they broke the hold of the feudal classes: 'only bourgeois rule tears up the roots of feudal society and levels the ground on which a proletarian revolution is alone possible'.[1] Now it was the turn of the workers. They were exploited, alienated and sunk in increasing misery. But for them to get their turn would not be easy. The capitalists owned the property, controlled the law, dominated art and literature and philosophy. 'The proletariat goes through various stages of development.' First, there are the 'individual labourers' and then 'the workpeople of a factory'. Next, the workers organize the 'operatives of one trade, in one locality' on the way to becoming 'concentrated in greater masses'. They go on to form broader 'combinations', particularly trade unions. They continue further to the 'organisation of the proletarians into a class, and consequently into a political party'. They are joined by intellectuals who desert the bourgeoisie, although 'the proletariat alone is a really revolutionary class'. Within the political party, the 'Communists...are...the most advanced and resolute section of the working class' and the communists have 'the advantage of clearly understanding the line of march'. The line of march is to the inevitable revolution.[2] 'Economic conditions had first transformed the mass of the people of the country into workers. The domination of capital has created for this mass a common situation,

[1] Karl Marx, *Class Struggles in France*, London: Lawrence and Wishert, 1942, p. 45.
[2] All quoted from Marx and Engels, *Manifesto of the Communist Party*, pp. 23–26, 30.

common interests. This mass is thus already a class against capital, but not yet for itself. The interests it defends become class interests. But the struggle of class against class is a political struggle.'[1]

The political struggle is subject to careful timing. The revolution must wait for the proper objective conditions as determined by those who understand the 'line of march'. The place is important as well as the time. The place is the city, not the country.

The small peasants form a vast mass, the members of which live in similar conditions, but without entering into manifold relations with one another. Their mode of production isolates them from one another, instead of bringing them into mutual intercourse.... the identity of their interests begets no unity, no national union and no political organisation, they do not form a class.[2]

The revolution was of workers in the towns, not of peasants in the countryside. Mass concentration of workers was a prerequisite, and so also was good communication—the railroad, for example, made the revolution easier and more certain. Agitation was the match that finally lit the fires of the revolution of the workers coagulated into the masses versus the classes, the Proletariat versus the Bourgeoisie. In the end it would all become international, and it was the 'workingmen of all countries' who were to 'unite'. Industrial crises and wars created the specific occasions when the world could be won.

The workers, since the Manifesto of 1848, have not gained the world. They have, however, often gained quite

[1] Marx, *The Poverty of Philosophy*, p. 145.
[2] Karl Marx, *The 18th Brumaire of Louis Bonaparte*, New York: International Publishers (no date), p. 109.

a lot else in the industrialized countries—but increasingly as citizens rather than as class-conscious workers.

2. As seen from a more modern viewpoint than that of Marx, the conflict over class has largely dissolved. Instead of six classes or five or two, there are said to be none at all in the Communist world—all men are equal and some are more equal than others; and, in the capitalist world, there are such infinite variations and gradations that it is better to speak of interest groups or status positions rather than class at all in the sense of a class set apart by its common attachment to grievances or to privileges or to a common ideology—all men are unequal and some are more unequal than others.

Morality attaches more to individual men than to classes, although there are now those who would urge a special moral position for the intellectuals.[1] Evolution is leading towards an all-pervasive middle class—a middle class that expands its coverage so widely that it is no longer a class at all. There are few hard and fast lines in this middle group but, rather, many minor grades that shade off into one another; except that an 'under-class' may be clearly distinguished and is in some places more visible where it has a special racial composition, as in the United States. The under-class stands outside the embrace of the great productive 'middle' segment.

Conflict is not concentrated at one place and at one time—at the barricades that separate the proletariat and the bourgeoisie. Friction is spread around in the ball-bearing society that has evolved. Protest is fractionalized. It is not over property but over countless prices and rules.

[1] See J. K. Galbraith, *The New Industrial State*, Boston: Houghton-Mifflin, 1967, p. 380.

It is not against the capitalist alone, but also against the merchant and bureaucrat and politician. The evolution of industrial society has helped this. There are fewer isolated masses in the lumber camp or textile town or mining village with common grievances against a single source of authority. The one-industry community is less frequent, and employer paternalism gradually passes away. Workers are concentrated into larger communities but these communities are so heterogeneous that the individual and the group are absorbed and contained and subdued.[1] Conflict is everywhere and this saves it from being anywhere to a degree that causes revolution—it is too scattered over time and place.

Marx saw a process that went on stage by stage until its ultimate conclusion—but the process stopped at about the stage he saw and went little further. Workers coalesced into trade unions and in some capitalist countries into political parties, but the trade unions remained bread-and-butter trade unions and the political parties remained cooperating political parties, and neither became revolutionary instruments. In England, at the time of the General Strike, and in the United States, with the I.W.W.s, it looked for a time as though the process might go on as Marx saw it, but the process was arrested. The process of developing increasing group consciousness stopped at the stage of economic trade unions and participating political parties.[2]

[1] See Clark Kerr and Abraham J. Siegel, 'The Interindustry Propensity to Strike', *Labor and Management in Industrial Society*, New York: Doubleday, 1964.

[2] Already in 1871, Marx 'found himself. . . now without the active support of the British trade unionists'; the unions, instead, embraced the 'politics of advanced liberalism'. (Henry Collins and Chimen Abramsky, *Karl Marx and the British Labour Movement*, London: Macmillan, 1965, pp. vii and 286.)

Relations of workers and employees became less violent, not more. Real wages rose. Trade unions developed power and influence in the work place— enough to get better rules and to settle grievances; and in individual industries—enough to be concerned with the profitability and growth of 'their' industry. As Bendix has noted, 'the willingness of entrepreneurial classes to compromise may increase along with the capitalist development'[1]—not hold steady or decrease. Political parties with worker support came to rule governments. Marx never thought that the capitalists would yield so easily the authority he believed they had over the state— for this, to him, was 'suicide'. The state turned to welfare. The law was, to a degree, impartial and was not just a tool of the dominant class.[2] Many buffers were created between contending parties. The 'new economics' of Cambridge replaced the old. Slichter once wrote of the crucial race between the engineer and the union leader, the one pushing greater productivity and the other higher money wages. A far more important race was between Cambridge economists and the great depressions, and Cambridge won—as Marshall had hoped it would in his Inaugural Lecture when he had called for 'training in thinking out hard and intricate problems, a training which is most rare in the world and plentiful only in Cambridge'.[3] The hard and intricate problem of counter-cyclical policy was solved.

3. Marx was wrong about the evolution of class in

[1] Reinhard Bendix, *Work and Authority in Industry*, New York: Wiley, 1956, p. 438.

[2] For a discussion of how 'citizenship' came to be more important than 'social class' in Britain, see T. H. Marshall, *Citizenship and Social Class*.

[3] A. Marshall, *The Present Position of Economics*, p. 56.

maturing capitalist nations. He expected revolution from the workers during an industrial crisis as the standard case. Communist revolutions have come instead more from the peasants and from war. Peasants to Marx represented 'barbarians' rather than civilized men. That they should have been important in Russia and particularly China and Cuba would have surprised him. Through foresight or by chance, however, he envisioned a war between Germany and Russia which 'will act as the midwife to the inevitable social revolution in Russia'.[1] But Russia was not an advanced capitalist nation and thus fell outside his central theory.

Communism has appealed less to the stage of late capitalism and more to early development than Marx had thought it would.[2] It has had a special appeal to people undergoing the transition from a traditional to a modern society. It speaks to their sense of revulsion against the old dynastic elite or against foreign domination. It speaks to their sense of exploitation. It speaks to their increasing sense of misery as they face the psychological impact of the 'revolution of rising expectations'. Communism, also, has some answers to the problems of the transition— control by the state, a social plan, fast capital accumulation. It is less well adapted to the complexities of an advanced industrial society where many small decisions must be made, and where individuals and groups achieve a degree of independence. Thus, in a world marked by many

[1] Marx and Engels, *Selected Correspondence*, Letter 147, p. 301. For a general discussion of the situation in Russia see Karl Marx and Friedrich Engels, *The Russian Menace to Europe*, edited by Paul W. Blackstock and Bert F. Hoselitz, Glencoe: Free Press, 1952.

[2] Engels did note this possibility in 1884. (See Seymour Martin Lipset, *Political Man*, Garden City: Doubleday, 1960, p. 68.)

countries in the early transitional stages into industrialization, Marxism has come to have substantial influence even though it has little appeal in more advanced societies.[1]

Marx saw revolution as the culmination of an historical process that pitted the workers, whose situation was deteriorating, against the capitalists. This it has not been. Hannah Arendt saw revolution more as 'restoration or renovation'[2] of lost privileges taken away by a despot (as by Batista in Cuba), the search for a more Golden Age like the one thought to reside in the past. Crane Brinton saw revolution as 'born of hope' in societies on the 'upgrade economically before the revolution came',[3] as was Russia. James Davies has suggested that revolutions arise from long-term economic and social improvements followed by a 'sharp reversal'.[4] Tantner and Midlarsky have expressed this as a theory of a period of rising 'aspirations' and 'achievements' followed by a sharp break in achievement as aspirations continue to rise, and a 'revolutionary gap' results.[5]

Among these theories—and with the advantages of historical perspective—it can be said that the process as seen by Marx least well explains Russia and China and

[1] Kaldor has observed that Marx, quite generally, understood better 'capitalism at the stage of transition from a pre-capitalist to a capitalist society' than he did the 'later evolution of capitalism'. (Kaldor, *Essays on Economic Stability and Growth*, p. 246.)

[2] Hannah Arendt, *On Revolution*, New York: Viking, 1963, p. 30.

[3] Crane Brinton, *The Anatomy of Revolution*, New York: Random House, 1952, p. 264. Alexis de Tocqueville also made this point: 'Evils which are patiently endured become intolerable when once the idea of escape from them is suggested.' (*The Old Regime and the French Revolution*, Garden City: Doubleday, 1955, p. 177.)

[4] James C. Davies, 'Toward a Theory of Revolution', *American Sociological Review*, February 1962.

[5] Raymond Tanter and Manus Midlarsky, 'A Theory of Revolution', *Journal of Conflict Resolution*, September 1967.

Cuba. Arendt can explain Cuba and Brinton, Russia. Davies best explains them all—a sharp reversal after an upward trend, as in the case of a disastrous war following a period of peace or a hated dictator following on the heels of a more benevolent system. But a sharp reversal did not lead to revolution in Germany and Japan after defeat in World War II. I would conclude that a communist revolution is most likely after a sharp reversal (military, economic, or political) takes place in a nation undergoing the transition from the traditional to the modern—and even then it needs strong leadership facing weak leadership. It may, of course, also occur as the result of conquest. But it never has come spontaneously from the workers against the capitalists in an advanced industrial society.

4. Marx—the prophet of the historical process—became the patron saint of one-third of the world as the result of historical accidents. He was a poor prophet but became a useful saint—for almost anything his followers may want to do finds some support in something he once wrote. But it still remains a mystery how 'a doctrine so illogical and so dull can have exercised so powerful and enduring an influence over the minds of men, and, through them, the events of history'.[1]

Marx would have been more nearly right about more of history if he had followed up on two of his passing thoughts—his thought about the consequences of a war between Germany and a largely peasant Russia; and his observation about England in that last chapter on 'The Classes'—that 'middle and transition stages obliterate even

[1] John Maynard Keynes, *The End of Laissez-Faire*, London: Hogarth, 1926, pp. 34–5.

here all definite boundaries'[1] between the classes. The first was an observation that lay outside his analytical framework. The second he rejected as 'immaterial for our analysis' since the 'tendency' was for a clear separation of classes.[2] The tendency, in all developed industrial societies has been just the opposite—towards obliteration of 'all definite boundaries'.

Marshall, on the whole, was more nearly right about the conflict over class. But again he would have been even more clearly right about England if he had paid more attention to the perverse 'class consciousness' of the British worker which he noted so parenthetically. Class collaboration has been little more the clear consequence of advanced capitalism than class conflict, and few legions march behind the banners of collaboration.

We inhabit instead an in-between world of contained conflict—contained by law, contained by the moderation of the parties, contained by the mechanisms for conflict resolution, contained by the limited aspirations of the claimants, contained by the willingness to compromise. There are thousands of battles, not one; and they are over authority, not ownership; over rising income, not increasing misery. The workers have not won the world, but as citizens they have achieved more political influence, more income, more security, more education. We have more nearly the 'laboristic state' of Slichter[3] than the communist society of Marx or the atomistic society of Marshall. The class gives way to group interests, and so does the perfect market.

[1] Marx, *Capital, Volume Three*, p. 1031.          [2] *Idem.*

[3] Sumner A. Slichter, 'Are We Becoming a "Laboristic" State', in *Potentials of the American Economy* (edited by John T. Dunlop), Cambridge: Harvard University Press, 1961.

# CHAPTER 5

# TRADE UNIONS AND
# GROUP INTERESTS

1. Marx looked at the unions from the viewpoint of class; Marshall from the viewpoint of the market. Marshall looked at them long and hard; Marx hardly at all. To Marx, unions were a passing phase of development on the way to the revolutionary proletariat. However, they could get in the way of the 'line of march', and particularly in Britain. At best, unions 'fail generally from limiting them-selves to a guerilla war against the effects of the existing system, instead of simultaneously trying to change it'.[1] At worst, the British working class ended up in the hands of 'corrupt trade union leaders'[2] who stood in the way of revolutionary development.

To Marshall, unions were a puzzle. They were both good and bad, and always complex. Marshall was the first labour economist of note and might even be called the greatest of all in the English and American traditions. More has flowed from his concerns over a longer period of time than from anyone else, more than from the Webbs or Commons or Marx. Marshall took an interest in almost the full sweep of what has come to be defined as labour economics and had important things to say in several areas. He was, as we have seen, interested in the evolution of the working class. He devoted much of the original volume entitled *The Economics of Industry*, with Mary

[1] Marx, *Value, Price and Profit*, p. 94.
[2] Marx and Engels, *Selected Correspondence*, Letter 168, p. 356.

Paley Marshall, to a discussion of trade unions. His *Principles* and the later *Economics of Industry* are much concerned with wage determination and the impact of trade unions. Along the way, he discussed labour markets, hours of work, labour productivity, collective bargaining and dispute settlement, and made major contributions to opening up the field now known as manpower development or manpower economics. Adam Smith and John Stuart Mill, of course, had similar interests, but they were less fully developed.

2. For his time, Marshall was amazingly friendly towards unions. Unions had earlier been held to be illegal combinations and were still greatly suspect in the period of the New Unionism in the 1890's. Employers and the public were hardly reconciled to them. Yet Marshall clearly was—with reservations.

Trade unions, above all, were an endeavour at 'self-government'[1] and, as such, they encouraged 'self-respect'.[2] They brought out the business and inventive resources of the workers. Along with the cooperatives, they raised the stature and the experience of the workers.

They aided not only democracy but also morality and this was, of course, most important: 'Unionism must be judged mainly by its influence on the character of the workers.'[3] Unions should encourage 'efforts to giving men a new spirit and a trust in and care for one another'.[4] In particular, they could fine each other to penalize 'excessive drinking'; and they should 'do what they can to make labour honest and hearty'.[5] The unions themselves

[1] A. Marshall, *Economics of Industry*, p. 187.
[2] A. Marshall, *Principles*, p. 703.
[3] A. Marshall, *Economics of Industry*, p. 388.
[4] *Ibid.*, p. 389.     [5] *Ibid.*, p. 391.

should follow 'the dictates of morality directed by sound knowledge'.[1] 'Mutual assurance'[2] was a worthy activity, and so was the training of youth in a trade. These were the non-economic impacts of unions, and they were all good.

Economically unions could overcome exploitation: 'the tacit agreements among employers would continually be broken through, and wages would rise and profits would fall nearly to their Normal level'.[3] Unions could protect against evil conditions and abuses generally and thus off-set the tendencies of 'bad masters'.[4] They brought shorter hours, and this was favorably viewed. Their impact in raising wages was salutary if it raised efficiency. 'A rise in wages almost always leads to an increase of Personal capital',[5] which was good, and it also could force out obsolete methods by making them too costly, which was also good.[6] The Common Rule was acceptable if it led to 'true standardization of work and wages'[7] among workers of equal efficiency.

This all sounds like a brief for trade unions. On the other side, Marshall weighed these disadvantages: restrictions on output and entry to the trade; wage bargains set at other than the 'normal' levels the market could justify; standard rates that put 'relatively inefficient workers in the same class for payment as more efficient workers'[8] or that kept the elderly out of work or otherwise added to

[1] A. Marshall, *Economics of Industry*, p. 403.
[2] *Ibid.*, p. 190.
[3] *Ibid.*, p. 200.
[4] Pigou (ed.), *Memorials of Alfred Marshall*, p. 214.
[5] A. Marshall, *Economics of Industry*, p. 202.
[6] *Ibid.*, p. 390.
[7] A. Marshall, *Principles*, p. 706.
[8] *Ibid.*, p. 706.

the Residuum—'refusing to allow an elderly man, who can no longer do a full standard day's work, to take something less than standard wages' was particularly 'harsh and anti-social'.[1] He disliked opposition to piece rates or insistence on inflexible piece rates—Marshall was particularly supportive of piece rates. He opposed violence and an excessive number of strikes (although a reasonable number of strikes was both necessary and desirable).

Marshall drew a clear balance sheet on the trade unions—as combinations they were all right; as combinations in restraint of trade they were not. Association was not bad *per se*. The test was the conduct *in* association. Unions sometimes exasperated Marshall, and bricklayers' unions in particular: 'If bricklayers' unions could have been completely destroyed twenty years ago, I believe bricklayers would be now as well off and more self-respecting' but 'cottages would be 10 or 20 per cent larger all round'.[2] But 'trade-unions...have exercised on the whole a liberating and elevating influence'.This judgment could be passed in part because the 'Masters' fought the 'restrictive influences'[3] of unions—their bad deeds were challenged and their good deeds were welcomed; and a union policy of restraint could remove 'nearly all the evil that still remains in the policy of unions'.[4] Unions above all should resist the 'temptation to go counter to the economic forces of the time',[5] and they could do this if they would only follow 'the dictates of morality directed by sound knowledge'. In the end he concluded that the 'pro-

[1] A. Marshall, *Principles*, pp. 707 and 708.

[2] Pigou (ed.), *Memorials of Alfred Marshall*, p. 400.

[3] *Ibid.*, p. 384.

[4] A. Marshall, *Economics of Industry*, p. 212.

[5] *Ibid.*, p. 389.

gress of the working classes' and the 'growth of Trade-Unions' had kept pace with each other.[1]

3. Thus spoke Marshall, more favourably than most observers of his day and of today as well. Today, at least in the United States, less attention certainly would be paid to the impact (if any) of the unions on morality, to the device of Mutual Aid now that the state has taken over so much of this type of activity, and to union resistance to effective piece rate systems now that piece rates are increasingly abandoned and, where still used, are so frequently based on agreements with the workers and set with more technical competence. More emphasis would be placed on the contribution of the unions to a sense of consensus in industrial society, to the sense that the rules and rewards are just and acceptable, and to how they thus lead to social tranquility.[2] This may well be their one great justification. It is easier to get the appearance of economic justice than to be certain about its reality—and the unions give the appearance. More attention is also now given to any impact of the unions on inflation, which was not a problem in Marshall's day—quite the contrary. The major new elements to be thrown into the balance sheet that Marshall drew are the impacts on consensus and on inflation.

4. To what extent have unions 'gone counter to the economic forces of the time' in the setting of wages? Marshall's views on this question stand the test of time

---

[1] A. Marshall, *Economics of Industry*, p. 362.

[2] It is recognized that strikes do occur, including strikes involving crucial public services, and that workers do from time to time repudiate agreements reached on their behalf. Yet the overall impact of unionization has been to contribute a sense of fair play, a sense of acceptance of the arrangements of industrial society.

exceedingly well. He saw three impacts—aside from the setting of the standard rate itself. First of all, union wages were somewhat higher than non-union wages,[1] but he made no claim that this was by any substantial margin. He noted the impact of non-union competition, the substitution of alternate products, and the substitution of machinery as off-setting forces. Second, the clear case for union impact on wages was in the craft area. The most successful method of raising wages was to 'limit the numbers in their trade'[2] through 'cruel apprenticeship regulations'.[3] The circumstances that he set forth in the *Economics of Industry* as most favouring artificially high wages all fit the craft case:[4] no substitute labour available, an inelastic demand for the product, the labour cost involved constituting a small percentage of total cost, and difficulties in the way of others getting the same benefits and thus spreading the costs.[5] The third impact was on money wages in a depression which were made more sticky in a downward direction.[6]

Marshall had some astute observations on the wage setting process under collective bargaining. 'If the employers in any trade act together and so do the employed, the solution of the problem of wages becomes indeterminate'[7] within limits. In a bargaining situation, the terms

[1] A. Marshall, *Economics of Industry*, p. 393.

[2] *Ibid.*, p. 211.

[3] Pigou (ed.), *Memorials of Alfred Marshall*, p. 385.

[4] *Ibid.*, p. 362.

[5] See discussion by Lloyd Ulman in 'Marshall and Friedman on Union Strength', *Review of Economics and Statistics*, November 1955, on how craft unions are inter-related and thus one craft pulls up another craft, and consequently the situation is not so different from that in industry. Essentially, however, Marshall and Friedman are correct in their views.

[6] A. Marshall, *Principles*, p. 709.

[7] *Ibid.*, p. 627.

are 'theoretically arbitrary'; 'in practice, however,' the parties 'will probably be governed by a desire to "do what is right"' which meant a little extra if profits were good and a little less if bad, but generally agreeing on 'payments that represent the normal earnings'.[1] And he added that 'there is *de facto* some sort of profit-and-loss sharing between almost every business and its employees'.[2] Beyond this, wages also responded to 'custom'.[3]

Marshall saw the one great shift in wage structures that has been verified in country after country over a long period of time, and this was the reduction of skill differentials,[4] but he did not relate this to trade union action.

Marshall saw the wage setting process as one of great complexity, particularly on the supply side, and he did not believe that the 'net influence of Unions on wages' could 'be clearly traced'.[5] He concluded, however, that 'the power of Unions to raise general wages by direct means is never great' and 'the direct influence of Unions on wages is small relatively to the great economic forces of the age'.[6] The market had its way: 'the main body of movement depends on the deep silent stream of the tendencies of normal distribution and exchange' and, by comparison, the organized actions of employers and employed are but a 'succession of picturesque incidents and romantic transformations' that are 'apt to be exaggerated'.[7] Long before the 'wage-drift' became a pheno-

---

[1] A, Marshall, *Principles*, p. 626n.
[2] *Ibid.*, p. 627.
[3] *Ibid.*, p. 560.
[4] *Ibid.*, p. 716.
[5] A. Marshall, *Economics of Industry*, p. 391.
[6] *Ibid.*, pp. 396 and 393.
[7] A. Marshall, *Principles*, p. 628.

menon of conscious importance, he wrote: 'You will need to watch the vast net-work of by-paths by which, when one person is willing to sell a thing at a price which another is willing to pay for it, the two manage to come together in spite of prohibitions of King or Parliament, or of officials of a Trust or Trade-union.'[1]

5. Several decades and countless studies later, the wisdom of Marshall largely stands. The standard rate has replaced personal rates in unionized and many non-union employments and has certainly often gone beyond, as Marshall feared it would, equalizing the rates of workers of equal efficiency; and it has brought greater equality among firms that lie within its orbit. It is amazing how wide apart can be the rates for the same type of work on the same product in the same area in the absence of the standard rate. In the United States, at least, the standard rate has helped to reduce or eliminate the wide geographical differentials that once marked this country. The other overwhelming change in wage structures has been the narrowing of occupational differentials,[2] particularly because education has placed more workers in skilled categories as Marshall foresaw. To this observation of Marshall's may be added two additional notes. First, inter-industry differentials have also narrowed slightly[3] because they are to a degree based on skill differentials. Second, unions may have impeded this process rather than aided it, despite the announced 'solidarity' policies of some, because of the conservative effect of the more formal wage

[1] 'The Old Generation of Economists and the New' in Pigou (ed.), *Memorials of Alfred Marshall*.

[2] See OECD, *Wages and Labour Mobility*, 1965, p. 34.

[3] See Lloyd Ulman, 'Labor Mobility and the Industrial Wage Structure in the Postwar United States', *Quarterly Journal of Economics*, February 1965.

relationships that they develop.[1] Union actions often solidify historical relationships and reinforce 'custom'.

Clear advantages are shown in the American studies, as Marshall would have expected, to a closed shop in the labour market and a high profit position in the product market. Doctors and building trades workers particularly have benefitted from restricted entry to the trade, and building workers' wages are in the high grouping as against the medium grouping in other countries where the closed shop does not apply. Restriction of entry may have advantaged these two groups to the extent of 20–25 per cent. And high profit firms and industries pay the higher wages. Restricted competition in the labour market and in the product market are the best assurances of sectional wage advantages. Again, as Marshall saw, money wage rates under trade union influence have held relatively steady in a depression. Keynes based his *General Theory* on the assumption of their constancy.

These basic aspects of wage behaviour are still as Marshall saw them. In two areas, however, his views require some modification. In the United States, trade unions have had rather more impact on union-non-union differentials than he might have expected.[2] Unions include only about one-quarter of the labour force and thus might be expected to have more of a differential impact, as

[1] See Clark Kerr, 'Wage Relationships—The Comparative Impact of Market and Power Forces' in John T. Dunlop (ed.), *The Theory of Wage Determination*, London: Macmillan, 1957.

[2] H. Gregg Lewis has concluded that unionism has raised 'the average relative wage of union labour' by 7 to 11 per cent in the early 1960's but by as much as 21 to 34 per cent in the special case of airline pilots. (*Unionism and Relative Wages in the United States*, Chicago: University of Chicago Press, 1963, pp. 194 and 293.)

Phelps Brown has noted,[1] than in England where more of the total wage structure is covered by more formal union relationships. But, as Marshall noted, the impacts of unions cannot be 'clearly traced'.

The second area is the role of the market. Wage surveys in the United States, particularly beginning with World War II, turned up astounding differentials within discreet labour market areas. It appeared that wages, rather than tending to be equal in such situations, were certain to be unequal. Yet this is exactly the situation where the market should be most effective—the same job in the same industry in the same labour market area. Dispersions were often of the order of twenty-five per cent or more between the highest cluster and the lowest cluster with two or three central clusterings and no clear 'market rate'.[2]

Yet the market, in other respects, seems to work quite well. Occupational differentials have responded to the long-term shift in the supply and demand situations for skill. The 'wage-drift', particularly in circumstances where there is some inherent flexibility, as in piece rates,[3] has made a mockery of hold-the-line wage policies except in

[1] E. H. Phelps Brown, *Minutes of Evidence*, No. 38, Royal Commission on Trade Unions and Employers' Associations, May 24, 1966.

[2] A forthcoming study by George Shultz of the University of Chicago and Albert Rees of Princeton will show that some and even many of the apparent discrepancies can be explained, on careful scrutiny, by the differing nature of jobs and workers, and that the market is thus more effective than it appears to be on the basis of less careful analysis. It should be noted that Marshall acknowledged that there were situations, particularly for manual labourers, where the market of its own accord yielded indeterminate results.

[3] For a discussion of the circumstances which favour the wage-drift see H. A. Turner, 'Wages: Industry Rates, Workplace Rates and the Wage-Drift', *Manchester School*, May 1956; and Turner, 'More on the "Wage Drift" ', *Manchester School*, January 1960. See also D. J. Robertson, *Factory Wage Structures and National Agreements*, Cambridge: University Press, 1960.

the short-run and under exceptional conditions. The market has reflected the massive forces of education and excess demand, but it has not, of its own accord, equalized local market rates.

Here is an anomaly. The market, which is a micro-institution, has been least effective at the micro-level and most effective at a more macro-level of adjustment. It is a certain sign that the local market has *not* been left to its own devices when rates are equalized for comparable work and workers; it is a sure sign of intervention by the state or the union. The market can make the massive adjustments of reducing occupational differentials or raising money wages in an inflationary situation, but it cannot equalize money wages in the local labour market. Local imperfections and rigidities are too powerful and 'normal distribution and exchange' too weak. The market has reflected the 'great economic forces of the age' but it has not dominated the local transactions and set a single 'normal level'; there is no exact equilibrium wage, no standard of normality in the 'free' labour market. 'True standardization' comes neither from the market nor from the union.[1]

Marshall requires modification on this score. Wages can 'drift' in response to excess demand,[2] and differentials

---

[1] The market does seem to work better—in the sense of equalizing rates—for more educated and mobile groups, like accountants and engineers, than for less educated and mobile groups; and thus, as education and mobility spread, the market historically will become more effective.

[2] The 'wage drift' has a bad name because it is the way to escape control in an inflationary situation. The 'drift', however, does make possible essential short-run adjustments in the 'scale' and the 'scale' is necessary for many institutional reasons in relations among unions, among employers, among government agencies—the 'drift' makes the formal scale viable. The 'drift', also, is one basis for long-run adjustments in the scale to keep it up to date.

can narrow with increased supply of skill, while wage ranges rather than a 'normal' rate characterize local markets. In the contest between 'market' versus 'power' forces, it is a mistake to assume that either can dominate the other as a universal rule. The beginning of wisdom is to know what the market can and cannot do, and what power can and cannot do. They both have their limitations. 'When one person is willing to sell a thing at a price which another is willing to pay for it, the two manage to come together in spite...of Parliament...or Trade Union' or even the Market. Local imperfections are too strong for the market, and the market is too strong for Parliament.

Two notations need to be added to Marshall, along with the two modifications. The first concerns the impact that unions have on the form that added benefits may take. For example, shorter hours, under union pressure, take the form of vacations with pay and even 'sabbaticals' in the United States, with enormous consequences for ways of life and the rise of new trades and industries, as compared with the consequences of further piecemeal shortening of the work week. As a further example, the impact of negotiated retirement plans, and health and welfare plans, in the United States has also been very great on ways of life and responsive economic activity.[1] The unions have probably had very little impact on the general level of real wages, but they have had substantial influence on the forms the benefits have taken. This was not seen by Marshall. Second, unions can, and under some circum-

[1] These plans were generally negotiated when the labour force was getting older. Now that the labour force is getting younger and thus more interested in current benefits, the union impact on the form that benefits may take, as against normal practice of employers in the labour market, may be lessened.

stances do, make wages more flexible upward during prosperity, as well as more inflexible downward during depression. Marshall saw a long period of stable or even falling prices in Great Britain and was not concerned about inflation. The modern age most definitely is. How concerned Marshall would have been about rising prices with money wages rising faster than productivity, of course, cannot be known, although he did once say he favoured a 'steady upward tendency in general prices'.[1] However, the problem would have been largely new to him.

In the new world of inflation, Marshall probably would have thought that trade union action would make inflation worse, just as it did deflation in the older world of periodic depressions; and he would have urged 'restraint' and doing what is 'right'. More flexibility under deflation would have been matched by more restraint under inflation. There would again be a place for 'morality' and 'sound knowledge'.

7. Marshall knew so much about labour markets, and yet he knew so little. He had an intense interest in and great knowledge about wage rates in the work place. He was one of the early supporters of better labour statistics. He was so wise in his comments about the sale of labour, about the 'exceptions' that are 'frequent and important' to the conditions that govern most commodity markets, about the error involved in 'regarding the labour market as like every other market'.[2] He emphasized that while 'the worker sells his work' he still 'remains his own property',[3] and thus his great interest in the conditions

---

[1] *Official Papers*, p. 9.
[2] A. Marshall, *Principles*, pp. 335 and 336.
[3] *Ibid.*, p. 560.

under which his 'work' is used—for the 'seller of labour must deliver it himself'. He was so clear that the true reward of an occupation was not just the money wage it paid but rather the 'net advantages'[1] after everything had been weighed. His statements on these matters are classic, in the sense of being fundamental.

But he overestimated mobility in response to 'net advantages'—the 'quick influx of youth' from other occupations when the advantages of any one occupation 'rise above the average', and how, 'when the advantages of a grade have risen...many small streams of labour, both youthful and adult, will begin to flow towards it'.[2] The main obstacle to mobility he saw was the tendency of the son to follow his father's trade. He also saw a reluctance to 'leave old associations'.[3] Marshall, however, generally assumed great mobility within an occupation and also among similar occupations. He deprecated the concept of non-competing groups as defined by Mill and Cairnes. Mill had spoken of the 'line of demarcation' that amounted almost to 'an hereditary distinction of caste' that divided the four great non-competing groups: the liberal professions, the artisans and the tradesmen, the skilled workers, and the unskilled labourers. Marshall thought these 'broad lines of division' as seen by Mill 'have been almost obliterated'.[4] Marshall, as a consequence, had a vision of *the* labour market within which there was great mobility vertically and horizontally. He expected and thought he saw the results in wages for comparable work being equalized by the market.

[1] A. Marshall, *Principles*, p. 73.
[2] *Ibid.*, p. 217.
[3] *Ibid.*, p. 567.
[4] *Ibid.*, p. 218n.

Many labour market studies have been made, particularly in the United States, since World War II.[1] Two major modifications must be made to Marshall's view, and they are so major as to make the Marshallian view an ideal type rather than a realistic model. To begin with, universal schooling has reduced the one great impediment that Marshall saw to mobility—the tendency of a son to inherit his father's trade. But there are other impediments. First, workers are much more attached to their particular jobs, to their friendships, to their seniority, and have much less knowledge of other possibilities than Marshall thought. They are much less actively in the market and pursue 'net advantages' less aggressively. The job contract, as Boulding once remarked, is more like a 'marriage'[2] contract than a bill of sale. The more realistic concept of labour mobility is that most people most of the time respond more to a 'push' than to a 'pull', and the Marshallian model depends on pulls.

Second, there are more institutional barriers than Marshall noted. Labour markets are 'balkanized'.[3] The craft is a 'guild' and the factory is a 'manor'—skill (reinforced by union rules) confines movement within the one, and seniority (also reinforced by union rules) within the other. Consequently there are many markets, not one; and within any market, the hunt for 'net advantages' is

[1] For an excellent summary of these studies see Charles A. Myers in Dunlop (ed.), *The Theory of Wage Determination*.

[2] In *Impact of the Union*, edited by David McCord Wright, New York: Harcourt, Brace, 1951, p. 254.

[3] Clark Kerr, 'The Balkanization of Labor Markets' in E. Wight Bakke, *et al. Labour Mobility and Economic Opportunity*, New York: Wiley, 1954. See also John T. Dunlop, 'Job Vacancy Measures and Economic Analysis' in *The Measurement and Interpretation of Job Vacancies*, New York: National Bureau of Economic Research, 1966.

not hotly pursued.[1] The dock worker and the carpenter, the employee of General Motors and the employee of Ford live in different orbits. Any movement between them is a source of surprise.

There is no such thing as *the* labour market, and also no such thing as *the* market rate. There are many markets, often only slightly connected with each other and sometimes not at all, and many rates with few of them precisely determined by any market. The normalities of Marshall are the abnormalities of the real world. He advised to 'take careful account of all the advantages which attract people generally towards an occupation'.[2] He should also have advised careful account of all the barriers that inhibit the pursuit of 'net advantages'.

8. Marshall had great concern for productivity. He was as opposed to the 'work fund' approach of the workers as to the 'wages fund' doctrine of employers; and it is interesting to note how the employers have given up adherence to their 'fund' more than the workers to theirs. Marshall attacked 'artificial work jurisdiction', opposition to better methods and machinery, restrictions on pace of work and output—obstruction of efficiency by the workers in every form and every guise. The problems he saw are of at least as great importance today; the answers he gave—essentially 'morality' and 'sound knowledge'— almost as ineffective.

Two additions can be made to Marshall's treatment. First, restriction of output is common among unorganized workers and less the sole result of unionism than he thought.

[1] The hot pursuit of 'net advantage' is more likely to be at the group level— as one organized group tries to achieve or exceed for all of its members the advantages secured by another related group.

[2] A. Marshall, *Principles*, p. 23.

In fact, union participation may ease the acceptance of more effective techniques, as well as impede it. Productivity has grown as fast since unionization as before, or faster; and productivity has advanced as much in union as non-union areas. Second, the craft situation is quite different from the factory; control by craft workers over the hand process is generally more effective than attempted control by industrial workers over the output of the machine. Also, management has less inherent authority in the craft system. In the United States, at least, restriction of output is largely confined to the crafts, and union action is not, in total, a net factor of substantial importance.[1] Group selfishness, in this area, has had rather minor impacts.

9. Marx and Marshall alike feared group interests: Marx, because they could get in the way of class consciousness on the way to revolution; Marshall, because they interfered with the market on the way to welfare. Marx feared and largely ignored group interests. Marshall feared but examined them most helpfully. Both would have been surprised—Marx, that class did not overwhelm group in the historical process; Marshall, that the market was not more effective in certain situations. Marx thought better of revolution and less well of ameliorative action by groups than the record now warrants. Marshall thought better of the market and less well of group 'selfishness' than reality now seems to justify. Group interests have not been on the 'line of march' to revolution, nor on the road to universal monopoly and restriction.

[1] For a similar conclusion about Great Britain see H. A. Turner, 'Memorandum to the Royal Commission on Trade Unions and Employers Associations', February 1967.

Marshall once wrote of the growth of 'sectional interests' and 'solidarity'; and feared 'grave and far-reaching injuries to the common weal'.[1] The capitalist world is now inhabited by 'sectional interests'. It is a world that lies in between the free market of Marshall and the 'social plan' of Marx.

[1] A. Marshall, *Industry and Trade*, p. 394.

# CHAPTER 6

# MARSHALL AND MARX
# AND MODERN TIMES

1. Marshall has a neglected side—the side that confronted the same concerns that were so important to Marx, concerns about the institutional context of economic activity and the evolution of society. I have sought to explore his disregarded views by contrasting them with those of Marx on a range of issues relating to the development of capitalism. Thus I have noted the common commitment of both Marshall and Marx to the classless society and the perfectibility of man; their disagreement about the future of capitalism—whether it might survive or not; their differing opinions over the inevitability of class conflict and the desirability of class collaboration; and their common suspicion—for quite different reasons—of 'sectional interests'.

Marshall in all his writing seldom mentioned Marx, although he was quite conscious of him and may even have had in mind that he was refuting him; and Marx never noted Marshall at all, but he was familiar with the views for which Marshall stood for they generally coincided with those of John Stuart Mill and the other 'vulgar economists'; yet Marshall and Marx may be said to have engaged in a great historical debate over the future of economic society. Who has turned out—on balance—to be more right and more wrong in this great debate? It is a debate which continues to this day with new facts, different contestants, a fresh jury.

2. One test of a theory is its ability to predict. Marx is

particularly subject to this test, for he wrote in his preface to *Capital* that he saw the historical processes that work 'with iron necessity towards inevitable results'.[1] Joan Robinson has noted how modern economists have had to turn toward some of the preoccupations of Marx, particularly 'monopoly and unemployment'.[2] Maurice Dobb has said that 'what must, surely, strike one as remarkable today is how very much more right he was than other nineteenth century economists and how much of his picture corresponds to leading features of our twentieth-century world'.[3] And Wassily Leontief once wrote of 'an unsurpassed series of prognostications fulfilled, against which modern economic theory with all its refinements has little to show'.[4]

Marx was right about some 'inevitable results'—the importance of the historical process at large as against what was happening in individual markets, the significance of class relations in understanding certain social developments, the central role of capital accumulation in growth and of growth to economic performance, the major significance of the phenomenon of depression, the trend towards concentration of economic activity in the industrial sector, the basic impact of increasing mechanization and division of labour, and the historical tendency towards a declining rate of profit in a period when capitalism was getting established.

But Marx was also wrong. Classes have merged, not

[1] Marx, *Capital, Volume One*, p. 13.

[2] Robinson, 'Marx on Unemployment'.

[3] Maurice Dobb, *On Economic Theory and Socialism*, London: Routledge and Kegan Paul, 1955, p. 201.

[4] Wassily Leontief, 'The Significance of Marxian Economics for Present-Day Economic Theory', *American Economic Review*, March 1938 (supplement).

separated, in developed capitalist societies. Evolution has taken the place of revolution. Affluence has increased instead of misery. The oppressive state has become the welfare state. The machine has aided man more and injured him less than Marx had thought. Depressions have become subject to control. The past century has seen both an economic and a political miracle occur.

Marx saw but rejected some forces that turned out to be very important—democracy, the welfare state, the trade unions, the peasants. He also neglected nationalism. He noted the differences between the Irish and the English, and the English and the French; and even wrote about the 'National Differences of Wages'.[1] But his theory neglected national history, national characteristics, and national institutions. He likewise neglected the possibility that revolution was more likely in early capitalism than in late. Yet the rise of nationalism and the instability of the developing nations have written much of the history of the past half-century.

There have been no 'inevitable results' and thus there was no 'iron necessity'. Marx was occasionally right about certain processes (like industrial concentration) but generally wrong about results—and the really important phenomenon has been the general results of capitalism.[2]

3. Were the Marxian predictions really 'unsurpassed', for example, as against those of Marshall? Marshall saw no 'iron laws'. Instead: while 'economic analysis and general reasoning are of wide application, yet every age and every country has its own problems; and every change in social

---

[1] Marx, *Capital, Volume One*, p. 611.

[2] 'As a prophet Marx was colossally unlucky and his system colossally useless.' (Paul A. Samuelson, 'Marxian Economics as Economics', *American Economic Review*, May 1967.)

conditions is likely to require a new development of economic doctrines'. He added that if any proposition 'points to any prediction, that must be governed by a strong conditioning clause in which a very large meaning is given to the phrase "other things being equal".'[1] He worried that his *Principles* would end up as 'waste paper'.[2] And Shove says that Marshall would have agreed with Wildon Carr's motto that 'it is better to be vaguely right than precisely wrong'[3]. Marshall was both.

He was right about many things: that the machine was on balance a blessing to the worker, that skill levels would rise, that real wages would increase, that trade unions and democracy could aid the lot of the worker, that a major source of advance was investment in human capital, that the trend towards concentration of economic effort in the industrial sector would continue, that a Residuum was a continuing problem. He was right, globally, in seeing a progressive evolution of capitalism. Stigler once noted, with less than full approval, that 'Almost every important subject in the *Principles* receives its exposition in terms of evolutionary change'.[4] Capitalism did evolve much as Marshall thought it would.

Marshall was also wrong. He neglected depressions and mass unemployment, and had faith that equilibrium at full employment was the natural tendency of capitalism. He saw socialism, rather than the welfare state, as the alternative to capitalism, and he feared it. He saw monopoly as the alternative to free markets, and largely neglected the

[1] A. Marshall, *Principles*, p. 37n.

[2] Quoted in Homan, *Contemporary Economic Thought*, p. 272.

[3] Shove, 'Place of Marshall's *Principles*'.

[4] George Stigler, *Production and Distribution Theories*, New York: Macmillian 1941, p. 62.

vast range of activity that falls between these polar situations. He put too great a faith in local labour markets in
equalizing wages. He had too great an expectation of
collaboration between capital and labour. He dealt too
much with opposites—like capitalism versus socialism,
and free enterprise versus monopoly—to the neglect of
the great variety of endeavours that occupy the territory
in between.

Contrary to Marx—Marshall was generally right about
results but occasionally wrong about processes. Overall,
however, it would seem that Marshall surpassed the
'unsurpassed' record of Marx. Marshall was generally
right about the future of capitalism and the working class;
Marx was in major respects precisely wrong. Marshall's
'Victorian complacency and gentility'[1] was superior to
Marx's 'dialectical materialism' in predicting the future of
advanced capitalism.[2]

4. We can say that Marshall was right and Marx wrong
about the progressive evolution of capitalism as we see it
in the 1960's. We could not say this as late as the 1930's.
The issue was then still in doubt with the 'great depression' holding sway and with bitter labour-management
disputes, particularly in the United States. The great
virtues of the Marshallian approach were almost buried by
its great fault—the neglect of mass unemployment. The
event that marks a clear victory for progressive evolution
was the *General Theory* of Keynes and its subsequent
acceptance as a basis for economic policy. In the 1930's,
depression, stagnation, class conflict were still major

---

[1] Viner, *The Long View and the Short*, p. 251.

[2] Marshall as modified by Keynes 'provided a fairly accurate method of
predicting'. (Henry Smith, *The Economics of Socialism Reconsidered*, London:
Oxford University Press, 1962, p. 122.)

elements of capitalism. Lange once wrote that Marx was superior in his understanding of the 'economic evolution of capitalist society', including depressions, and that the 'bourgeois' economists, which meant Marshall among others, were superior in their understanding of the 'everyday life of a capitalist economy', including the operation of markets and the setting of prices.[1] Now in the 1960's the 'bourgeois' economists understand depressions, and it is the economists of the communist nations who have turned their attention to an attempted understanding of markets and prices. Marshall was wrong about depressions, and Marx was wrong about the labour theory of value. The followers of Marshall now understand more about depressions than do as yet the followers of Marx about prices.

5. Marshall and Marx need not have been so wrong. Much of what happened could have been seen, in fact was partially seen and dismissed, by both Marshall and Marx. What can we learn from their efforts at predictions? I should like to suggest these rules:

(1) To look again at what any system of analysis rejects. Marx should have looked again at the peasants and also at the British workers; Marshall, at depressions.

(2) To beware of taking a single force—like the mode of production or the strength of the market—to its logical conclusion, for there may be countervailing forces. That something could happen does not mean it will happen, and particularly not in its entirety. The mode of politics can guide and even control important elements in the mode of produc-

[1] Oscar Lange, 'Marxian Economics and Modern Economic Theory', *Review of Economic Studies*, June 1935.

tion, as democracy has guided capitalism; and men individually and collectively can and sometimes do resist the force of the market. This means being doubtful of unilinear historical processes, like the inevitable triumph of the workers or even of education and morality. Being aware that something could happen may even mean that it will not happen.

(3) To be alert to the in-between situations—like the welfare state or monopolistic competition—as against the concentration on opposites.

(4) To know that problems do not necessarily get worse. They often give rise to solutions. Solutions do not necessarily get better. They often give rise to problems. Men emerge from their caves of despair but never enter the doors of Utopia.

(5) To accept human nature as possibly improvable but not perfectible in any system, and technology as improvable in every system.

(6) To realize that the recent past is not the future. It never has been and never will be. Neither the 1850's nor the 1870's held within themselves all of the future; nor do the 1960's. The future is a very long time in which we are all dead.

Men continue to make predictions, and the power of a prediction that people like and believe or dislike and still believe can be enormous. This is one of the main lessons of Marx. Thought and action can be separated, contrary to Marx, but often they are not. Thus there exists great power in some predictions and some views of the social totality—as there has been in those particularly of Marx but also of Marshall.

6. The predictions and world views of Marx and

Marshall were developed under the special circumstances of their times. They sought to understand existing circumstances and they sought to prescribe solutions to the problems they thought they saw.

They saw the rise of the factory system. Workers were the great new class. These workers were developing their economic and political instrumentalities, and establishing their goals. Aside from the workers, the other great new force was that of the capitalists—the entrepreneurs who owned and controlled and managed, and who were a growing element in ruling society as well as the plant. These capitalists were heavily oriented towards profit. Economic life was becoming dominant over religious and social life; becoming the overwhelming preoccupation of the people. The state was as yet rather primitive, largely concerned with protection against enemies abroad and disorder at home. Education, particularly at the higher levels, was for the hereditary elite. Agriculture was being superseded by industry, and agriculture and the people engaged in it were neglected by both Marshall and Marx as vestiges of a dying system. Religion was still a great influence in the daily lives of the people and Victorian morality was basic to the conduct of the family and the teachings of the school. Intellectually, it was a period of optimism—the century of Utopian thought; a period when new possibilities, new horizons were being explored; when the classless society seemed possible and man was inherently good and confidence in the future was triumphant.

Marshall and Marx sought to understand this world; to understand how the new workers would behave and also the new capitalists and the new state; how economic life might influence all of man's behaviour; how the new goals of men might draw forth new responses. They sought to prescribe for this new world—to prescribe the free market that would bring wealth and welfare for all, or to prescribe the revolution that would usher in the classless society where man could realize the full potentialities of his inherent perfection; to prescribe the economic arrangements that would permit men to live the good life of 'gentlemen' without 'chains'.

Both Marshall and Marx left an historical residue of understanding and prescription. The new liberalism was overcoming the old *status quo* and Marshall helped to liberate the new liberalism. Workers were rising as a new element and Marxism helped draw attention to the importance of the workers; and the realization of their importance helped lead to their absorption into society, helped encourage the formation and acceptance of their unions and cooperatives and labour parties. The new liberalism made possible the acceptance of the workers and their organizations; the new socialism made this possibility an urgent necessity. Thus these contrasting approaches, represented by Marshall and Marx, made progressive contributions *together* to the new synthesis of modern society where the workers were integrated within the framework of liberalism. Marshall and Marx, with their understandings and their prescriptions, in open contemporaneous conflict yet unwitting historical cooperation, helped shape modern capitalism. They also gave rise to Keynes and to Tito—to guided capitalism and to market socialism; and thus to potential reconciliation between the worlds of capitalism and socialism.

7. The liberalism and socialism that helped shape the current *status quo*, however, both now stand historically

exhausted.[1] New facts require new understandings and new prescriptions.

The factory loses its importance to the shop and the office and the classroom and the research centre. The newer classes are those of the service workers, and the white collar employees and the bureaucrats and the students and the technicians and the intellectuals; each establishing their own instrumentalities and their own goals. The capitalists share their once central role with the politicians and the private managers and the public administrators and the scientists and the professionals. More tests than profits alone animate performance of the big enterprise, for there are also tests of contributions to welfare and of image and popularity. Economic life shares more of its former dominant position with the political life of the community, and both with the sensate and existential life of the individual. The state has found new dimensions of activity in welfare and greater participation, and become more responsive to more elements of society. Education is reaching into additional layers of society and changing the capacities and aspirations of people as it does so. New goals are being born that go beyond economic welfare and materialistic proficiency.

New problems have arisen—unseen by Marx and Marshall: problems of inflation rather than deflation, of affluence and its consequences within developed societies rather than misery, of nationalism that gets in the way of both the international community of the working class and the world market of the capitalists, of population

---

[1] 'Marxism suffers the fate of liberalism: it is found wanting as a theory of post-bourgeois society.' (George Lichtheim, *Marxism*, London: Routledge and Kegan Paul, 1961, p. 394.)

increase, of the rise of the underdeveloped world with the increasing misery of its rising expectations that makes relations between the underdeveloped and developing and developed worlds rival in their importance to the evolution of world society the significance of the internal structures of the developed world that so preoccupied Marx and Marshall.

New solutions have been explored beyond the more effective market and beyond more aggressive working class action as roads to salvation: through group action as well as that of the individual and the state, through the welfare state rather than the capitalist state or the socialist state, through contained conflict rather than class conflict or class collaboration, through an infinity of status differentials instead of either class or classless relationships, through pressures at work within a pluralistic system as well as the impacts of morality or of revolution, through muted group advantage as well as profits or selfless contribution, through group bargaining as well as the market and the plan, through rapid evolution as against the *status quo* or revolution, through a 'live and let live' policy as against the all-out warfare of one sectional interest versus another.

New means, new goals, new views are all at work. The new technology creates new functions, and new groups to carry out the new functions; it makes possible new goals; gives rise to new views, new options to men. The task of today, however, is basically not so different from that of Marx and Marshall: it is to understand the new forces and prescribe the new solutions one century later. A great struggle is once again engaged to create the effective understandings of the new situation and the operative new prescriptions. The new understandings and new programmes for action will be both post-liberal and post-socialist; post-Marshall and post-Marx. They will transcend both liberalism and socialism. The time is too late and the circumstances too different for either or both of these earlier ideologies. Marshall and Marx reflected their time and their place. The new understandings and solutions need to reflect the new times and new places.

The world of today is an in-between world from those seen by Marshall and Marx for the advanced capitalist societies. Marx saw England when the urban slums were being born, when women and children were going to work in the factories, when the right to vote was not yet universal. Marshall saw England when the sun never set on the Empire, when there was free trade, when there was a gold standard. In the century that intervenes, a new world of 'group-action, of collective control, massive competition and mass bargaining'[1] has grown up. The structure of society has changed. What is it like? What are the new irreversible processes and 'inevitable results'? What are the new possibilities for prescriptions under human control? I should like to examine these questions from the point of view, as noted earlier, of an American pragmatist and pluralist in the 1960's. I shall begin by noting some of the various current ways that have been proposed for looking at modern capitalism as it has evolved and is evolving. In doing so, I realize how greatly people can disagree about the nature of our economic system of today, just as Marshall and Marx did about the capitalism of their day; for we are still trying, quite imperfectly, to understand, as did they, where we are, where we may be going, where we should be going.

[1] Shove, 'Place of Marshall's *Principles*'.

73

CHAPTER 7

# INDUSTRIALISM AND PLURALISM

Capitalism in its modern form is neither what Marshall or Marx thought he saw, nor what either of them really wanted. Marshall wanted a further unfolding of individual rationality and morality in an ever upward evolution; Marx, sharp and sudden change in a working out of the dialectical process toward the achievement of collective rationality and morality. Instead, the actual development has been more that of the 'growth of a branching tree'[1]—branching into new directions and new forms. New understandings and new solutions need to reflect the new times and new circumstances.

The society that has evolved has been called many things. It has been seen in different ways by different people. Its essential features have been quite variously described:

To Slichter,[2] as we have seen, the United States, at least, has evolved from a capitalist to a 'labouristic state' where the interests of employees and the actions of their organizations are the 'principal influence'. To Hicks,[3] the 'labour standard' has replaced the gold standard. The Webbs and Commons had earlier described the rise of the organizations and the goals of labourers to a dominant place in society.

[1] Talcott Parsons, 'Wants and Activities in Marshall', *Quarterly Journal of Economics*, November 1931.

[2] *Op. cit.*

[3] J. R. Hicks, 'Economic Foundations of Wage Policy', *Economic Journal*, September 1955.

## Industrialism and Pluralism

To Dahrendorf,[1] Western Europe and North America have become 'post-capitalist' societies where inter-group tensions have replaced class conflict, and the new 'service class' of white collar or black coated workers and bureaucrats sets the tone. This was the earlier vision also of Weber and Schumpeter.

To Rostow,[2] the United States, in particular, but other countries as well, have entered the stage of 'high mass-consumption', with the automobile as the particular symbol of this stage. To Johnson,[3] some Western economies may now be identified as the 'opulent society' in which the 'masses are becoming capitalists' and the central problem is the 'evolution of demand as wealth increases'; and Galbraith[4] once wrote of the 'affluent society' geared to private consumption. In France, a frequent reference is to the 'consumptionist' society.

To Galbraith,[5] the new 'industrial state' is dominated by the actions of a few hundred large corporations, under the leadership of the 'techno-structure', that control their own capital and product markets and work closely with governmental agencies. The more or less independent 'educational and scientific estate' also develops greater influence and holds within itself the capacity for leading evolutionary change. The 'techno-structure' actually manages society on a daily basis; the 'educational and scientific estate' may guide it into its future. The demise of the older entrepreneurial system has

[1] Ralf Dahrendorf, *Class and Class Conflict in Industrial Society*, Stanford: University Press, 1959; and 'Recent Changes in the Class Structure of European Societies' in *A New Europe?* (edited by Stephen Graubard), Boston: Houghton-Mifflin, 1964.

[2] W. W. Rostow, *The Stages of Economic Growth*, Cambridge: The University Press, 1960.

[3] Harry G. Johnson, 'The Political Economy of Opulence' in *Money, Trade and Economic Growth*, London: Allan & Unwin, 1962.

[4] John Kenneth Galbraith, *The Affluent Society*, New York: New American Library, 1958.

[5] Galbraith, *The New Industrial State*.

led Lichtheim[1] to speak of the 'post bourgeois' society; and Marris[2] of 'managerial capitalism' where the 'professional manager' becomes the key figure. Berle and Means had earlier noted the reduced role of ownership.

To Bell[3] the new society may be identified as 'post-industrial' where 'intellectual institutions' with their emphasis on theoretical knowledge become the central focus of activity rather than the factories as in earlier times, and where decisions are increasingly of a technical character. I have elsewhere written of the rise of 'ideopolis' as a centre for the life of society.[4] And Machlup[5] has described the rapid growth of the knowledge industry. Schumpeter had earlier viewed intellectuals as essentially destructive as compared with the more constructive roles assigned them in these more current views.

To Boulding,[6] the world is now entering the stage of 'post-civilized' society where technology keeps advancing steadily around the globe guided by the 'scientific ideology', and a new range of problems must be faced—particularly population increase and annihilating war. Along with this goes the 'organizational revolution'[7] with dominance by organized groups. Society of the future has also been identified as 'technotronic'—as constantly subjected to ever newer technology and particularly to electronics. This is the world that Marcuse[8] so detests—a world where the industrial system based on its new technology, and whether under capitalist or

[1] Lichtheim, *Marxism*.

[2] Robin Marris, *The Economic Theory of 'Managerial' Capitalism*, London: Macmillan, 1964.

[3] Daniel Bell, 'Notes on the Post-Industrial Society (1)', *Public Interest*, Winter 1967.

[4] *The Uses of the University*, Cambridge: Harvard University Press, 1963.

[5] Fritz Machlup, *The Production and Distribution of Knowledge in the United States*, Princeton: Princeton University Press, 1962.

[6] Kenneth E. Boulding, *The Meaning of the 20th Century*, New York: Harper, 1965.

[7] Kenneth E. Boulding, *The Organizational Revolution*, New York: Harper, 1953.

[8] Herbert Marcuse, *One-Dimensional Man*, Boston: Beacon Press, 1964.

communist control, takes away the 'inner freedom' of man; the 'one-dimensional' society where 'manipulation' replaces class conflict.

These views are illustrative of current efforts to comprehend modern society. They vary greatly from one to the other in selection of the key class or element: labour, the bureaucrat, the consumer, the professional manager and technician, the intellectuals in general, the scientists in particular; and in the key force at work: sectional gain, administrative rationality, consumer supremacy, corporate survival and growth, new ideas, new technology; and in tone: of the acceptance, however reluctant, accorded to labour, the bureaucrat, the consumer and the professional manager, of the hope, however muted, tied to the role of the intellectual, and of the fear, however exaggerated, tied to the role of the scientist. Solutions vary also from suggested restraint by labour and the consumer, to inevitably increased sophistication in the bureaucrat and professional manager, to intended liberation of the intellectual, to seizure of control over the scientist and over technology. These views vary greatly but they have in common the conviction that society is entering a new stage requiring a new understanding. They each reject some and even much of the inheritance from Marshall and Marx.

2. 'Pluralism', or more precisely 'pluralistic industrialism',[1] is another way of describing modern society. There may be said to be four major ways of organizing society:

[1] See Clark Kerr, John T. Dunlop, Frederick Harbison and Charles A. Myers, *Industrialism and Industrial Man*, New York: Oxford University Press, 1964.

the conservative, around community and personal leadership;
the classical liberal, around the individual, free choice and markets;
the pluralistic, around groups and organizations, and accommodation;
and the radical, around 'truth' and through the collectivity.

For industrial society, Mayo[1] and Tannenbaum,[2] among others, have stood for the first with the plant or the union local taking the place of the tribe and the guild; Marshall for the second; Madison and de Tocqueville and the Webbs and Commons for the third; and Marx for the fourth.

The realistic alternative as industrialism evolves, is some form of pluralism. Industrialism brings division of labour and mobility and large-scale organizations and conflict that destroy heavy reliance on community; it brings large-scale organizations, including the state, that reduce the atomism of a society once based on the small merchant, the handicraft shop and the family farm; it brings complexity and more education and diversity of interests that prohibit any permanent attachment to a single 'truth' and a monolithic system of organization of the Stalinist type. Societies converge towards pluralism— towards a reliance on markets and plans and group bargaining; toward several or even many centres of power rather than none or only one; towards infinitely complex mixtures of rationality and irrationality, morality and immorality, principle and pragmatism; towards many managers and even more who are managed; towards many conflicts over rules and rewards. The world of work is marked by the actions and inter-relations of individuals,

[1] Elton Mayo, *The Human Problems of An Industrial Civilization*, New York: Macmillan, 1933.

[2] Frank Tannenbaum, *A Philosophy of Labor*, New York: Knopf, 1951.

heterogeneous groups and governmental authorities of such diversity that it defies analysis by reference to any single force, whether the market or class conflict; or to any single element, whether labour or the bureaucracy or consumers or professional managers or intellectuals or scientists.

Pluralism accepts a sphere for individual and group independence in the face of technological interdependence. It allows partial communities to exist within the larger society. Industrial pluralism, based on a variety of semi-autonomous enterprises and associations, recognizes that there must be a central political authority, which was the difficult point for the earlier political pluralists who had tried to envisage a society with ultimate power divided, and thus industrial pluralism accepts the state with final coercive authority subject to checks and balances and limitations. The community, the individual, the group and the organization, and the state are all accepted and accommodated to varying degrees.

Pluralism is no single entity, by its very nature. It covers a very wide range of arrangements. I should like to suggest four points of concentration within this span:

'coordinated pluralism' which is more or less held together by a single doctrine and central leadership, as in modified communist societies like Yugoslavia;

'managerial pluralism' which is more or less held together by the accepted policies and common interests that loosely affiliate the leaders that manage the major entities, as in the United States;

'liberal pluralism'[1] where there is a conscious and consistent

---

[1] See Clark Kerr, 'Industrial Relations and the Liberal Pluralist' in *Labor and Management in Industrial Society*, New York: Doubleday, 1964.

effort to free individuals from excessive group domination while accepting the absolute necessity of group organization and cooperation among groups; and

syndicalism where the group becomes autonomous—and presumably democratically structured internally—with little or no central coercive authority, with each group free to go its own way, with special emphasis on the self-governing work unit.

Each of these four types of pluralism has within it great variations, a wide span of alternative structures. In the pluralistic world, the 'coordinated pluralists' (née communists) become the conservatives or even the reactionaries; the 'managerial pluralists', the moderates; the 'liberal pluralists', the reformers; and the syndicalists, the radicals.

The coming struggle for power, once industrialism has moved past its initial stages, will be among proponents of these four forms of pluralism. This is a struggle which can never be concluded. When the struggle was seen as over the ownership of property, that struggle had some possible ultimate solutions; so also over the purity of markets; but when it is over authority—since authority can never be held equally by all or entirely by one in the advanced industrial society—there is no pure solution.

I should like to turn next to my own brief description of 'mankind in the ordinary business of life'.[1] May I comment with great emphasis that an effort to describe and to analyze reality does not necessarily imply defense of it. May I also comment, once again, that the American experience, which I reflect, is to a degree unique but not therefore unimportant. American experience does show

[1] A. Marshall, *Principles*, p. 1.

a relatively 'pure' industrial situation since there is no feudal background and technology is the most advanced.[1] It is 'impure', however, in its background of slavery.

[1] S. M. Lipset, 'The Changing Class Structure and Contemporary European Politics' in *A New Europe?*, p. 338.

# CHAPTER 8

# THE MULTI-DIMENSIONAL SOCIETY

1. Modern society is marked by the activities of many groups engaged in many endeavours and with many loyalties and many styles of life. Multiplicity is its all-pervading characteristic. It is multi-form in character. It has many dimensions. At its heart is what I shall call the 'inner-society'. This inner-society includes what was once identified as the working class, by now an increasingly conservative element of the inner-society. Caught below this inner-society is an 'under-class'; and standing outside it are the 'outer-elements' of students and some intellectuals, and of the aged.

The inner-society is composed of the managers and leaders, workers and white collar employees, and the independently engaged professional and agricultural and craft personnel that constitute the great productive segment of society. It is comprised of the regularly employed, fully productive, fully accepted, fully protected members of society and their families. This inner-society is united by basic acceptance of the surrounding society and support of it, and there are no clear lines of internal cleavage. Tensions do exist within it but not the essential cleavages that Marx thought he saw; tensions among groups replace conflict among classes. The inner-society is increasingly integrated within the increasingly interdependent productive processes of society, absorbed within the great consensus,[1] cared for and consulted within the welfare state and the welfare corporation—there are no old bosses and no new masses. This inner-society keeps for its members most of the rewards and all of the status.

This is not to suggest that everybody in the inner-society knows that he or she is a part of it—but then the workers did not always know they belonged to what was once identified as the working class. However, members of the inner-society do know that they have a stake in the *status quo*, are given tasks to do that are deemed useful, are affiliated to a lesser or greater degree with the centres of power. Individually most members of this inner-society do not feel themselves part of a class; mostly they just want to be left alone and not put into any categories by anybody. The edges of the inner-society are fuzzy—young workers, part-time workers, workers in low-status jobs are on the periphery. The mass of the inner-society is also most varied in its nature—from industrialists to file clerks. But the inner-society does exist in the sense of a great group of people bound together by the relationships of productive effort, accepted and rewarded, without any clear class lines to divide them—only infinite gradations. Its members are part of the productive system, part of the empire of the 'establishment'.

2. At the centre of the inner-society in the United States are all the public and private governments under their leaders and administrators and managers. If there

---

[1] To work well, industrial society demands a basic 'necessary consensus' among its productive elements. (See Simon Kuznets, *Modern Economic Growth*, New Haven: Yale University Press, 1966, p. 500.)

can be said to be a single dominant centre, it is the federal government, not Wall Street—the federal government that unites and gives general direction; but there are many quite independent, even conflicting, centres of power. The state, the corporation and the trade union, however, no longer stand in such contrast to one another as they once did, either in form or in ideology.

Marx saw the state as the tool of the capitalists; Marshall saw the state as necessary and desirable but standing at the opposite pole from the entrepreneur in terms of its creativity and initiative. The state has become more a partner of capital and labour, and sometimes the tool of both; and more a promoter of growth than oppressor of initiative. Pigou once noted the role that the state was plying in research and innovative projects, and thought that even 'Marshall...might...have somewhat modified his verdict'.[1]

The large corporation, in turn, has become more like a private government and somewhat less like the 'firm' of neo-classical economics—a private government with its rules, its bureaucracy, its areas of control over capital sources and influence over product markets, its multiple goals of survival and growth and public image as well as short-run profits, its sense of 'professional responsibility'.[2] This has happened quite beyond the public utility and defense industry sectors; and thus it is generally helpful to view the large corporation of any type as a government as well as a firm. The ideology of industrial leadership has shifted from that of the entrepreneur

[1] A. C. Pigou, *Socialism versus Capitalism*, London: Macmillan, 1937, p. 87.
[2] Robert L. Heilbroner, 'The View From the Top' in Earl F. Cheit (Ed.), *The Business Establishment*, New York: Wiley, 1964, p. 9.

stressing ownership, profits and master-servant relationships to that of the manager arguing function, efficiency and human relations.[1] The business leader is involved in much more than just responding to the dictates of the market.[2] Now this view neglects the whole world of the small firm and the service trades which are growing so rapidly, but the large corporation sets much of the tone of modern industrial society. The 500 largest corporations in the United States account for nearly one-fifth of all employment.

The trade union also becomes a private government. The correct model of a trade union has long been a puzzle. A union can be many things. It can be an agent of the state as in a totalitarian system; it can be an agent of the employer as under company unionism; it can be an agent of revolution under radical control; it can be an agent of its class in a class society. But mostly, in modern capitalist society, it is the agent of its members. However, this does not settle how it will behave. It may follow an economic model, and sometimes does, maximizing the income of its members according to one or another definition.[3] But generally 'the stimulus to maximization afforded by business competition has no equivalent in the trade union case (unless the phenomenon of dual unionism can be invoked).'[4] It may follow a political model, and sometimes does, using the wage bargain as an instrument in conflict with another union

[1] See Bendix, *Work and Authority in Industry, op. cit.*

[2] See Robert Aaron Gordon, *Business Leadership in the Large Corporation*, Washington, D.C.: Brookings, 1945, pp. 3–12.

[3] John T. Dunlop, *Wage Determination under Trade Unions*, New York: Kelley, 1950.

[4] Lloyd Ulman, 'Union Wage Policy and the Supply of Labor,' *Quarterly Journal of Economics*, May 1951.

or among union leaders.[1] Mostly, however, it is a private government guided by bureaucratic leadership.

Public policy in the United States favours this managerial model. One union is given a monopoly on representation at any one time. And, also, most unions are one-party systems. Thus their leaders can act 'responsibly'; that is to say, like a 'benevolent bureaucracy'. They help make and administer the rules of industrial society; set the pattern of rewards. They are a functioning part of each of their industries; and related in many ways to governmental agencies. They are part of the *status quo* and help administer it. Unions take their place in the ranks of the private governments of industrial society.

Also taking a place of importance are the countless non-profit institutions which account for five per cent of the employment in the United States.[2]

The public and private goverments of industrial society are consenting partners in the establishment, as well as competitors and opponents. The state and the corporation and the union all accept each other. None seeks to destroy the other and all have a stake in the success of the system. Decisions are made more on the basis of formal rules or meeting a standard target or just getting 'more' than for the sake of fully maximizing returns in the short-run. Doing 'what is right' and 'custom', which Marshall saw as factors affecting wage determination, also determine much else. The participants are all interested in growth

[1] Arthur M. Ross, *Trade Union Wage Policy*, Berkeleu: University of California Press, 1948.

[2] Governmental and non-profit agencies together account for one-quarter of all employment in the United States, and nine out of ten new jobs between 1950–60 were created in these areas. (Eli Ginzberg, Dale Hiestend, Beatrice Reubens, *The Pluralistic Economy*, New York: McGraw-Hill, 1965, pp. 87 and 204.)

for the sake of power and survival, but mostly prefer to be in a 'passive' rather than an active state of aggression against or defense from some other group. They seek an optimum path of accommodation in the longer run. They act like benevolent bureaucracies or 'agreeable autocracies'[1] towards each other and the people they serve. The tests of conduct they must meet give some room for adjustment and accommodation. Thus there are areas of indeterminacy and there is room for bargaining. The 'compromise benefit' of Marshall finds its place in practice as well as in theory.

These consenting partners form no great conspiracy of the 'power elite'. There are those who see the 'establishment' as fully united, when in fact it is often divided; as frozen, when in fact it is open to persuasion; as impenetrable, when in fact new people and new elements constantly enter it. Within the 'establishment' there are many conflicts but these conflicts are played out within the rules of the game and with no thought of destroying the system but rather with an eye to its preservation. Within these limits the leaders generally represent their constituencies effectively.

Leaders are recruited, increasingly, from the same pool of talent, and structures are sufficiently loose so that people can and do move among industry, government, universities, and now occasionally even unions. Each of these institutions has its managers, and these managers have much in common. Increasingly they all have technical training and a professional point of view that turns disputes into problems to be solved. The experts

[1] Joseph P. Lyford, *The Agreeable Autocracies*, New York: Oceana Publications, 1961.

87

help settle the inevitable conflicts of interest on the basis of facts and analysis, and also with an eye to preservation of the existing system, rather than on 'principle' except for a general attachment to the concept of a reasonable and a balanced society. This inter-mingling and inter-communication of the technical experts greatly aids the working of the system. And considering the amounts of income and authority at stake and the vast amount of change to be absorbed, the system of accommodation works well.

One of the main tasks of the major and minor leaders of the public and private governments is to serve as inter-mediaries between their organizations and their members; as means of tying the 'centre' and the 'periphery' together.[1] The members often want more opportunity for participation than large-scale organizations easily afford, and the desire for participation is now sometimes so great that it can hardly be assimilated. The success of the inner-society, and particularly its stability, depends heavily on how well the middle elements of leadership associate the mass membership with the top leaders, on how effective they are in their political tasks of communication. Generally top leaders become more sophisticated in their techniques and middle layers of the bureaucracy better educated and more adaptable,[2] and thus the system works more smoothly.

The public and private governments led by their public

[1] Edward Shils in writing of the problems of the 'mass society' stresses the need for tying the center and the periphery together. See Edward Shils, 'The Theory of Mass Society' in *Diogenes* (An International Review of Philosophy and Humanistic Studies), Fall 1962, No. 39, pp. 45–66; and 'Center and Periphery' in *The Logic of Personal Knowledge: Essays presented to Michael Polanyi on his Seventeenth Birthday*, London: Routledge and Kegan Paul, 1961.

[2] See discussion in Michael Crozier, *The Bureaucratic Phenomenon*, Chicago. University of Chicago Press, 1964.

and private 'servants' keep a reasonable degree of harmony in a largely interdependent society, and at the same time introduce constant change. The process is less disruptive than the class conflict of Marx and less harmonious than the class collaboration of Marshall. The process is compatible with an advanced industrial system. In the United States it has worked far better within the inner-society, as I shall shortly note, than it has in relation to the under-class and the outer-elements.

Of necessity, there is an 'end' to an 'ideology'[1] of conflict within the inner-society. Older ideologies of class conflict within the productive process have become 'exhausted'; and issues, of necessity, are confronted one at a time on the basis of their individual merits. Economic ideologies have given rise to great disappointments, and cannot, in any event, comprehend the infinite complexities of modern industrialism. The time is past when heroic roles were given to the great entrepreneur or the humble worker, when passions swirled around their contributions to history.[2] Instead of the visible hand of the entrepreneur or the fist of working class instrumentalities, or the invisible hand of the market, there is now the largely hidden hand of the experts in the offices of government agencies, corporations, trade unions, and non-profit institutions working with cost-benefit analysis, with planning, programming and budgeting—and they often work together. While specific ideologies fade within the inner-society, an overall ideology of interests *versus* 'truth', of accommodation *versus* conflict, of slow change *versus* revolution is inherent in pluralism.

[1] Daniel Bell, *The End of Ideology*, New York: Free Press 1960.
[2] Edward Shils, 'The End of Ideology?', *Encounter*, November 1955.

The public and the private governments, under the leadership of the highly trained, seek pragmatic solutions to constantly new problems and possibilities. The public institutions hold more initiative than was once thought possible, and the private hold more of a sense of social responsibility. The view of the expert weaves them together in a loose confederation of restrained conflict and imperfect accommodation; weaves them together through the rules of reason and the rule of self-preservation, rather than a precise ideology.

Ideology may well have reached its 'end' within the inner-society. New ideologies, however, may come to rise from the under-class and even more likely from the outer-elements of the students and associated intellectuals. The old ideologies related to economic roles and processes are fading; new ideologies concerned with wider participation in decision making and with new patterns of life may be arising, bringing an early end to the 'end of ideology'. In particular, the economic system which was once viewed as too ineffective may come to be viewed as too successful and too dominating.

3. Access to the inner-society and position within it comes to be based less on hereditary privilege and more on education and ability. The degree taken comes to predict better than the occupation of the father the life history of the son, although there remains a strong relation between the degree taken and the education of the father even in the United States.

The amount of education available, its quality and its distribution become major determinants of progress in an industrial society. The United States now spends nearly seven per cent and soon will spend eight per cent of

Gross National Product on education, with the corresponding figures for higher education being two and three per cent. The educational system becomes, as Wicksteed noted long ago, a 'great sorting machine for adjusting opportunities to capacities throughout the whole population'.[1] But it is very hard to make education do its job really well. It not only selects but it rejects, and there is some evidence that it rejects the less disciplined who might be saved and the more creative who should be saved. Beyond that, the investment process is imperfect. Parents, as Marshall noted, vary in their ability and willingness to invest. Students often lack collateral and time perspective and are unwilling to assume the risks of investment in themselves. The state is troubled about availability of resources and whom it should assist. So the process of investment is, as yet, very imperfect.

The consquences of this imperfection are great. Life earnings and position in society are directly related to ability and to investment in human capital among individuals. Equality of opportunity to achieve life earnings and a position in society depends on equality of access to funds for education. Among entire societies, the less the equality of schooling, the less the equality of earnings[2] and thus the less the equality of position in life, as in the American South. The inequality of investment in human capital causes inequality of income and of quality of life. Inequality in income and power, which was once tied mainly to physical and financial capital, is now also tied to human capital. Here the rich may become

[1] Philip Henry Wicksteed, *Common Sense of Political Economy*, Volume One London: Routledge and Kegan Paul, 1933, p. 335.

[2] Gary S. Becker and Barry R. Chiswick, 'Education and the Distribution of Earnings,' *American Economic Review*, May 1966.

richer and the poor, poorer, and particularly if the poor pay taxes to educate the rich. There is still the challenge to see that 'inequality of income in one generation' does not also cause 'inequality in the next generation'.[1]

The educational system becomes central to the economic and social system. How many shall be educated? To what levels and in what fields? How shall they be selected and rejected? Educational relations take the place of class relations; the educational market that precedes becomes more important than the labour market that follows; conflict over educational opportunities replaces conflict over class roles. Education plays a particular role in determining who gets into the leadership group that manages the industrial system, that runs the public and private governments. In the United States today, educational opportunity has generally been equalized within the two top income quartiles; it has not fully penetrated into the lower two quartiles.

4. Education prepares people to approach the different ports of entry into the many internal markets that mark the industrial society—ports of entry for manual workers, clerical workers, technicians, professionals. Most movement is within these internal markets once entered; most of the working life of the population is lived within them.[2] These internal markets follow their own rules which are set by management and by unions largely at their own discretion. They are much more subject to institutional control than product markets, and are of a comparable level of importance.

Three general types of internal markets exist—those

---

[1] Pigou, *Socialism versus Capitalism, op. cit.*, pp. 21–22.

[2] In Japan, commitment to an internal market is a life-time contract.

based on the craft, where equality is the basic rule; those based on the factory, where seniority is the rule; those based on the office, where merit is the most basic rule. These markets vary greatly in their conduct, and each type has major impacts on the lives of the people within it. Each of these markets is partially insulated from the external market, and it may take major disjunctions with the external market to cause internal adjustments in rules, rate structures and assignments. There is usually substantial leeway for judgment in how closely internal decisions should follow the indications of the market. The external market, however, stands as a constant guide to what is reasonable internally and can force internal decisions; yet the internal market has a life of its own. The connections between internal decisions and the external market are a largely unknown territory.

The internal markets are tied to the external markets at ports of entry—apprenticeship for the craft, the bottom of the seniority list for the factory, and a whole layer of entry positions for the office. There are also ports of exit—the voluntary quit, discharge, retirement and death. The number of ports of entry and their location, the rules governing entry and exit, the nature of life between the ports of entry and exit are of great importance, for, as John Stuart Mill and Marshall insisted, 'the quality of a man's working life, his relations with other men in it, and the influence of his work on his character'[1] are the essential ingredients; and the internal markets of industrial society are the primary influences on working life. The achievement of industrial 'justice' is largely related to the conduct of these internal markets.

[1] E. H. Phelps Brown, 'Prospects of Labour', *Economica*, February 1949.

Education affects access. The internal market affects the quality of life. Marshall saw the former clearly; the latter, not so clearly. Marx saw neither. The life of industrialism is largely lived within the internal markets of the work place. The transactions there define the quality of economic justice. Membership in the inner-society for most people most of the time means life in one or another of the vast series of internal markets.

5. Progress no longer just happens. It is forced. Individuals and agencies specialize in it. In the United States today, Research and Development takes three per cent of the Gross National Product, and two of the three per cent comes from the federal government; higher education may soon take three per cent, not counting research and development funds; and new capital investment—much of it based on 'forced' savings by government, by corporate management, by private and public social security—accounts for fifteen per cent. Thus a total of one-fifth of the GNP is deliberately directed towards progress. Ideas and skill, and the new capital that embodies and uses both, make progress, to a degree, automatic and inescapable and even, to some, frightening. There develops what has been called 'the invention industry'.[1]

The role of the university becomes central—to basic research and the service related to it; to training and the talent hunt; to development and transmission of a general view of society; and to dissent against that society. Beyond the university rises the non-profit institution for

[1] Richard R. Nelson, Merton J. Peck, Edward D. Kalachek, *Technology, Economic Growth and Public Policy*, Washington, D.C.: Brookings, 1967, p. 44.

94

research and evaluation—Rand and Brookings and the Hudson Institute. The performance of the university, in particular, affects the progress of the nation. It moves to the centre of the stage and also to the centre of conflict; it becomes so important that no one wants to leave it alone—not just Henry VIII but now all the people. This is new.

The role of the intellectual also becomes more central—in the university, government, industry, the union, the non-profit institution. Intellectuals become more influential than is usually the case in a commercial or agricultural society, and much more numerous. This also is new.[1]

An advanced industrial society cannot decline absolutely; but rates of advance from one to another can vary enormously. They will vary depending, in part, on how well progress has been institutionalized. Advanced industrial societies become increasingly dependent on higher levels of skill in their people and technology in their capital. Society comes to move ahead not so much in response to the dynamics of class relations or even to the ever-present prodding of the market, but more in response to the pressures of institutionalized progress. The inner-society has made permanent the process of technological progress.

6. The first transformation of the working class came with its creation and its early existence as a force for reform—seeking better wages and shorter hours, acceptance of its organizations into the power structure

---

[1] 'The modern intellectual class in all its elaboration is a unique historical phenomenon.' (Edward Shils, *The Intellectual Between Tradition and Modernity*, The Hague: Mouton, 1961, p. 9.)

of society, full political citizenship for its members. The second transformation of the working class is its entry into the inner-society and embracement by it. Jobs get better. Income rises. Security is improved. Workers get the vote. Unions attain power. Workers and their institutions are no longer a class apart. Early flirtings with class consciousness, as the workers strove for reform, give way to acceptance and support of the inner-society as workers gain acceptance and influence.

The working class not only tends to disappear as a class-conscious and recognizable element in society; it needs to disappear if modern industrial society is to operate with full effectiveness. So must and do all other class-conscious groups within the productive segment of society. Class-consciousness leads to attitudes of class conflict which are incompatible with modern industrialism. This is realized by the practical men who head industrial societies. Workers become citizens under capitalism; comrades under communism; and patriots under nationalism.

The intricate and infinite decisions that must be made in an advanced industrial society require reason and compromise, and can only be made more difficult by class antagonism. Pragmatic solutions are possible; class justice is not. Also, small decisions are more feasible than large ones. Thus it is easier to set farm prices or wages within small segments than to determine the class shares of farmers or of workers. The effort to determine a class share can tear a society apart.

Class thinking gives rise to concepts of domination and exploitation, not adjustment and contribution. The 'wages fund' or the 'work fund' are class approaches to how much employers should pay or how much workers should work. They are lines across which people fight. Neither one is compatible with full growth and productivity. Modern industrial society is rather fragile; any one of many essential elements can immobilize it or at least seriously impair its function. It requires fundamental acceptance of its validity to make it work well. Thus the pragmatic approach replaces the theoretical, the small decision the large, the constructive solution the restrictive, and acquiescence replaces resistance to the system as such.

Fortunately, what is necessary is also likely. Modern industrialism tends to open up opportunities for upward mobility so that hereditary position is an influential but not a determining factor,[1] to bring greater equality of net income so that the poor get absolutely richer and the rich comparatively poorer, to create fine gradations of status from the bottom to the top of the hierarchy so that there is no clear line of demarcation, to set up mechanisms for consultation and sharing of decision-making so that authority is more widely dispersed. As a result, class-consciousness tends to be muted and finally to disappear. Any society where it continues to be an influential factor handicaps itself in the international competition among nation-states.

The working class as a self-conscious class—any self-conscious class within the productive system—tends to disappear, to succumb to euthanasia.[2] One test of an

[1] Glass found in England a 'good deal of upward and downward movement in social status between generations'. A little less than one-half fell from upper levels and a little more than one-half rose from lower levels. (D. V. Glass, *Social Mobility in Britain*, London: Routledge and Kegan Paul, 1954, p. 20.)

[2] The white collar group may well turn out to be more ideological

97

industrial society is how successfully it meets this require-
ment; one form of sabotage in any industrial society is
the preservation of class antagonisms. The classless society
is now not alone the goal of the Victorian moralist
or the scientific socialist, but also of all practical leaders
of all industrial societies. The inner-society absorbs within
its ample dimensions the prior classes of workers and
capitalists thrown up by early industrialism, and unites
them into cooperative economic production and consenting political citizenship.

The working class not only disappears, but the workers
become like everybody else on most issues most of the
time. On some issues, however, they tend to become a
relatively conservative element within the inner-society.[1]
They often oppose technological change. On issues like
race relations and international affairs, they also count
among the less progressive elements. Blue collar workers
come to be among the less tolerant strata of society[2] and
there may even develop a 'lower-class fundamentalism
and authoritarianism'.[3] Leaders in communist states come
to appeal to the workers and their organizations as a
force for stability as against the pressures for reform by

than the manual workers, and also harder to handle once organized, since their
organization generates more resistance from employers who think of white
collar workers as closer to management. As the white collar group rises in
size as against the blue collar workers, this becomes a factor of considerable
potential importance. (See George Sayers Bain, *Trade Union Growth and
Recognition*, Royal Commission on Trade Unions and Employers' Associations,
1967.)

[1] A large minority of workers in Britain have always been 'conservative
and thus conservatism is not a new phenomenon. (See Robert McKenzie and
Allan Silver, *Angels in Marble: Working Class Conservatives in Urban England*,
Chicago: University of Chicago Press, 1968.)

[2] Lipset, *Political Man*, p. 109.

[3] S. M. Lipset quoted by Shils in *Encounter*.

the intellectuals. Revolutions have come from the middle
class seeking democracy, dynastic elites taking refuge in
fascism, nationalists trying to eliminate colonial rule,
peasants looking towards individual ownership of land
but actually on their way into communism,[1] but not
from workers in advanced industrial states. The situation
of the workers constantly improves; and their organizations come to bargain with power at their command,
rather than lead revolts.

The workers once absorbed become more conservative
and their unions become more bureaucratic—another
agent of control in industrial society. The workers and
their instrumentalities together are no longer *the* agent of
change and sometimes not even *an* agent of change,
although they may still give allegiance for historical reasons to liberal or labour or socialist or even communist
parties, with the 'illusion' that 'the class struggle is still
going on',[2] and thus remain a force for reform.

In any event, the evolution of the working class
is not as central to social processes as once thought by
both Marx and Marshall; it is less of a liberating and
more of a conservative force. New elements of society
take the initiative—the leaders of the inner-society,
the students and some intellectuals outside, and the
dissidents from the under-class. The working class
belongs more to the old order; these other elements more
to the new. The working class is part of the inner-society
and less of a force there. The workers are no longer the
under-class on their way up. There is a new under-class.

[1] See Barrington Moore, Jr., *Social Origins of Democracy and Dictatorship*,
Boston: Beacon, 1966.
[2] George Lichtheim, *Marxism in Modern France*, New York: Columbia
University Press, 1966, p. 198.

7. Underneath and outside this great productive and protected community of the inner-society lies the new discontent of the non-integrated and the non-consulted. The existence of an under-class is both inevitable and troublesome, but not fatal as would be class divisions within the inner-society itself. It is inevitable because a tendency towards exclusiveness is inherent in the approach of the inner-society and its constituent groups—of some much more than of others. Some of the most basic rules of society govern who is admitted and who is rejected, and some of the most important mechanisms are concerned with selection—including the educational system. People are rejected on grounds not only of education but also of race and age and ability. Membership in the inner-society is defined by acceptance; in the under-class, by rejection. The under-class is troublesome because it can cause distress for the inner-society, but it can never conquer it.

Myrdal has spoken of the 'under-class' of the 'unemployed and, gradually, unemployable and under-employed persons and families' caught in a 'trap' at the 'bottom of a society'.[1] The very concept of an 'under-class' runs counter to the principle of equality of opportunity in industrial society. Yet it exists to a lesser or greater degree; a class not fully active in the labour market; not fully embraced in the productive process. The 'under-class' is the familiar Residuum of Marshall— 'the Residuum of our large towns'[2] made up of those 'incapable of doing a good day's work with which to

[1] Gunnar Myrdal, *Challenge to Affluence*, New York: Ransom House, 1962, p. 34.
[2] A. Marshall, *Principles*, p. 2.

earn a good day's wage' as well as 'some besides those who are absolutely "unemployable".'[1] The 'lumpen-proletariat' and the 'industrial reserve army' of Marx were similarly outside the productive process. As we have seen, Marshall wanted the Residuum to be 'attacked in its strongholds'; but it still exists and may even tend to grow. Marx thought the lumpen-proletariat and the industrial reserve army would disappear under socialism. The under-class has turned out to be, in the United States at least, a much greater problem than either Marshall considered the Residuum to be or Marx, the lumpen-proletariat; but less of a problem than Marx saw in the industrial reserve army of the unemployed which kept on growing.

The under-class exists because of lack of native ability, impoverishment of the surrounding environment, accidents of life. It exists also for 'artificial' reasons—because of the rules that the members of the inner-society create to protect themselves. The inner-society tends to be protective in its attitudes; and race and nationality and level of education and age can all become bases for protection. The inner-society sets up the groups with which it does not wish to associate—its list of 'non-competing groups'.

The 'standard rate' rules out all those who cannot meet the standard, as Marshall pointed out so long ago. A 'good day's work' at a 'good day's wage' keeps out those who might otherwise provide a less 'good day's work' at a less 'good day's wage'. The Marxian rule of 'from each according to his ability' comes to be defined as excluding those of low ability. Craft workers shelter

[1] A. Marshall, *Principles*, p. 714.

themselves behind apprenticeship and membership rules; industrial workers protect themselves with seniority. The employer wants workers who can justify the standard rate, the cost of hiring and training, the burden of health and retirement benefits; and he often prefers overtime for members of his own internal market to new employees drawn from the under-class. Hours of work are standardized also at a level that suits the standard worker better than the handicapped or the aged or the less disciplined. Formal rules on level of education and a 'clean record' stand as other barriers. Protection for the inner-society is exclusion for the under-class. The view from inside the gates is towards the morality of standards; from outside the gates, towards the immorality of exclusion and discrimination.

Thus there is the excluded under-class, always dependent on the inner-society for support and usually at poverty levels. Its members are excluded also from the organizations with real power inside the productive community. They have no representation at the council tables where the rules that govern the world of work are made.

The problem has become acute in the United States, and suddenly. Myrdal in 1962 wrote of the under-class there as 'not very articulate', 'not much noticed', 'not becoming organized'.[1] All this has changed. Other problems have been solved; other groups have been integrated into the inner-society; and the under-class now demands that its problems be solved, that it be integrated. The rebellion of the under-class comes not at a time when its lot is getting absolutely worse but when it stands on the threshold of getting relatively

[1] Myrdal, *Challenge to Affluence*, p. 39.

better. It is the prospect of advancement that encourages the under-class out of lethargy into a state of excitement; its temperament is generally more passive.

The under-class in America constitutes perhaps fifteen per cent or more of the nation.[1] Two overlapping factors contribute to this very substantial size: (1) racial discrimination affecting Negroes, Puerto Ricans, Mexican-Americans and Indians, and (2) geographical isolation in urban ghettos and in isolated rural areas like the Southern Appalachians and Indian Reservations. The centre of the discontent is now the ghetto in the metropolitan area where masses of people are congregated and share their sense of grievance. A true class-consciousness is developing there around race, and race can be a basis for class-consciousness as working class status turned out not to be. The other class movement in American history also came from the under-class of the migrant workers organized by the I.W.W. before World War II. Both of these class-conscious movements, arising from the under-class, have given rise to violence.

The under-class can rebel, but it cannot lead a successful revolution. The great city, it turns out, is subject to disruption on the streets—disruption by individual and collective action alike. Some of the disruption comes from conflicts within the ghetto itself, from Negroes and Puerto Ricans or Negroes and Mexican-Americans against each other; and not just from conflicts with the inner-society. Great city after great city has half or more of its residents to some extent involved in the under-class.

[1] Michael Harrington has used the figures of twenty to twenty-five per cent. (*The Other America*, New York: Macmillan, 1962, p. 182.) He includes the aged.

The city may belong almost totally to the inner-society during the day but partially to the under-class at night. The conflict of earlier times of the city versus the country finds its modern counterpart in the central-core *versus* the suburbs.

The new class conflict is in the ghetto as it never was in the factory. The ghetto is more subject to class-consciousness and to violence than the factory has ever been. The lines of demarcation between the ghetto and the surrounding society are more clear-cut than between the worker and the manager; and violence is a more natural weapon. In the factory, the worker can put on pressure by withdrawing his labour—even great pressure. The under-class has little to withdraw economically, although it can withdraw its votes politically. The factory provides channels of communication to centres of power, channels which are absent in the ghetto. Transactions between the ghetto and society can be through charity, through political organization and through non-violent or violent rebellion. Charity is distasteful; political organization not always effective; and thus rebellion is a natural recourse. Confrontation and force are used as dramatic ways to be heard through the nearly sound-proof curtain that surrounds the inner-society; but their effectiveness is reduced by the substantial fragmentation of the under-class itself.

Much can be done with and for the under-class and by the members of the under-class for themselves. The Scandinavian countries under the social democrats have greatly reduced anything that could be called an under-class. Their 'active labour market policy' concentrates on training and geographical movement. Marshall particularly wanted to save the children. Better health and better education are clear but long routes, and meet barriers of inadequate motivation and thus lagging achievement. More jobs, even subsidized jobs, under more welcoming rules, constitutes a shorter route being taken now in the United States by even those strongholds of self-protection—the construction trades.[1] The inner-society has long learned how to protect its more inept members and shows great tolerance of them and solicitude for them once they are accepted;[2] and so there is substantial possibility for absorption of members of the under-class into the inner-society without subsequent rejection, given sustained full employment.

Many immigrant groups, once discriminated against, have been integrated into American society. Much of the remaining under-class stands on the threshhold of this same process. An under-class will still remain but it can be reduced in size and raised in its condition until it is tolerable.

The problem of the under-class is endemic in modern industrial society and not an American problem alone—of persons not fully absorbed into the industrial system and protected by it, as is the case of foreign workers in Northern European countries since World War II, as the Irish once were in England, and as are persons on the welfare rolls of any large city.[3] Modern industrial societies

---

[1] The creation of ports of entry into the internal markets of the inner-society for members of the under-class has received great attention recently in the United States.

[2] William J. Goode, 'The Protection of the Inept', *American Sociological Review*, February 1967.

[3] As Pen notes, the Lorenz curves of income distribution are remarkably similar among industrialized societies with the bottom 20 per cent of the population receiving about 5 per cent of the income. (J. Pen, *Harmony and Conflict in Modern Society*, New York: McGraw-Hill, 1966, p. 39.)

tend, in quite varying degrees, to be dual societies—dual societies of the inner-society and the under-class.

8. Modern industrial society also has at least two outer-elements. One is composed of students, particularly at the level of higher education. In the United States today, there are over six million of them and by 1975 there will be nine or ten million. They stand outside the inner-society. Their youth and their position of freedom between earlier subjection to adult authority and later acceptance of adult responsibility make them, to a degree, a class-apart. They have no structured role in the world of work. They often have no position of authority on the campus itself. When great issues rend the surrounding society, some of these students constitute an especially volatile group, particularly if, as so often happens in the United States, they are concentrated on large campuses in metropolitan areas. They may even develop their own separate cultural patterns. The new means of communication draw them more into the affairs of the world and give them also more chance for expression of their own views. The political activists are always a minority, even a small minority, within the outer-element of the students—most students have inner-society attachments and values—but under certain circumstances may set the general tone for students as a whole.

Student dissent has been known throughout much of history, but it recently has taken new forms. Traditionally it has been against a repressive system, as in Czarist Russia, or oppressive paternalistic rules, as in the earlier history of Harvard. Dissent has been against remnants of the old feudalism and the old dynastic leadership in society and in the universities. Currently it takes place not only against repression—as, for example, against the new feudalism of communist societies—but also in quite permissive societies and quite permissive universities. Permissive institutions are not necessarily effective or moral or democratic; in fact, they may be inefficient, corrupt and bureaucratic.

The dissent of the students is against the new as well as the old—against the new pluralism and the impacts of the new technology. It is not basically materialistic in origin for it responds more to affluence than to personal depreviation. Nor does it as yet have a continuing ideological base in political theory as did the socialist movements of youth in the past. Instead of a carefully articulated socialist attack on the old order demanding more state control, there is an essentially non-ideological syndicalistic dissent against the new order demanding more individual participation. It is more existential in tone; more a response to moral outrage at arrangements and events in society—often quite unrelated arrangements and events; more a reaction to a sense of powerlessness, with influence in the family lying in the past, influence on the campus historically rejected, and influence in the inner-society not yet clearly in sight—in sum a reaction to psychological deprivation which is the new facet of 'increasing misery'. The combination of moral outrage and powerlessness to do much about it among many persons concentrated together and encouraging each other gives rise to the new phenomenon. A natural tendency of muted anarchism towards the surrounding society and of syndicalism towards their own associations results.

Associated with the students are some of the teaching

staff. Members of the teaching staff on the American campus are on the margin of many relationships, both partly inside and partly outside the inner-society; and intellectuals, by their very nature, have divergent tendencies among themselves and against society. Many faculty members are associated with the inner-society through their research and their consultation. Others— particularly younger members of the faculty and many of all ages in the humanities—stand outside. This sense of standing outside may be increased in future decades as the supply and demand situation starts turning against faculty members, and thus their comparative economic situation again deteriorates.

The rise of the campus as a centre of dissent is, to a degree, a world-wide phenomenon. Once the factories and the farms are no longer so much the focus of dissent, the campus and the ghetto take their place—partly by default; and university authorities become reluctant substitutes for employers and absentee landlords or even colonial administrators. And the campus is a fragile place dependent on its own internal tolerance and the money of the surrounding society. Marx and the Marxians discounted the political role of students since they were viewed as unreliable and not centrally located in society. Marshall saw students on their way to becoming gentle-men. They are now more centrally located than Marx once thought and less likely to view themselves as gentlemen-in-waiting than Marshall hoped.

Another new element is that the activist students now lead the external intellectual activists as well as the other way around. Historically there were student chapters of social movements in the surrounding society under adult leadership. Now the students also energize the liberal and radical intellectuals—they are more sensitive to the times, less bound to ideologies and institutions and responsibilities. The adult intellectuals now follow as well as lead—some quickly and fully, some slowly and partly, some now and then, and some not at all; but the energy and the mass base comes mainly from the students. The campus becomes the centre not only for its own locally generated dissent but also for dissent in society. The campus is a ready-made base for unrest—it provides facilities, a degree of autonomy, an audience, and recruits for dissent. Thus some students, some faculty and some intellectuals become associated with each other in dissent with the campus as their base and the students in a position of partial leadership. This happens, in part, because other centres of dissent in the church, the press, the political parties, the workers and the farmers become muted and absorbed into the general consensus of a pluralistic society.

This outer-element of the students and associated intellectuals is a more intractable problem than that of the under-class. It is subject to growth, not dimunition, and is inherently activist. Improvement of the economic lot of the student is no clear answer or any answer at all; and there are sharp limits to the integration of students into the life of the outside community and even into the governance of the campus. Also, and this was one of the theories of Freud, work lies at the basis of reality; and more and more young people spend more and more time outside the world of work. Society may need to accept more unrest from this direction as a permanent feature.

This unrest from the students is inherently hard to handle. The students are not part of 'the system' but stand outside it. To get the attention of the 'system' they turn, as do members of the under-class, to dramatic approaches including confrontation and the use of violence; they cannot have any impact by just withdrawing their effort as can elements of the inner-society. Students are hard to discipline—they stand outside the family and outside the penalties of the work place, and the campus is usually hesitant to use discipline. They are hard to integrate into the inner-society for they are not part of it; they cannot bargain within it; they have no continuing bureaucracy to be accommodated and absorbed; and, on campus, there are rather narrow boundaries to what the faculty and the administration can and will concede by way of participation. Nor can they be easily satisfied by higher incomes or higher prices. Their moral indignation and their sense of powerlessness are not subject to ready concessions. Thus students may tend to stand outside the inner-society and some of them confronting it for a long time to come.

Students and affiliated intellectuals, not the workers of Marx, may turn out to be an intermittent source of radicalism—radicalism is more intrinsic in their natures and they are less easily satisfied; and to be the chief locus of alienation towards the surrounding society. This outer-element has some of the characteristics that Marx thought he saw in the working class. It grows in size, and dissent is endemic within it. This was one of the great concerns of Schumpeter who feared that the intellectuals would gnaw away at the foundations of capitalism until it gradually faded away into socialism; that the 'host of intellectuals' with their 'hostility'[1] would help lead the 'march into socialism'.

[1] Joseph A. Schumpeter, *Capitalism, Socialism and Democracy*, New York: Harper, 1950, p. 153.

But student status is temporary; for a period of years, not a life-time. Thus students flow in and out; and when they flow out of student status most of them become part of the inner-society, often abandon their old causes and become more conservative—the opiate of students is age; alienation gives way to assimilation, a muted anarchism to an unconscious acceptance of pluralism. And both the students and the intellectuals are divided in many ways, by many interests, by many points of view. Intellectuals, in their totality, are also heavily integrated into the inner-society. Beyond this, students and intellectuals are to a degree erratic, subject to changing moods and styles, lacking in the endurance, for example, of an old-time trade union or working class movement; they flow in and out of consensus with the inner-society depending on the issues of the time and the nature of the top political leadership. Nor are they necessarily always more 'moral' than all the rest of society, more endowed with understanding. Additionally, even the integrated intellectuals are not in the real centres of power.

Thus the activist students and affiliated intellectuals serve more as a catalyst initiating concerns and ideas, more of an irritation to and pressure on the inner-society, more of an intermittently pulsating force depending on the gravity of the issues and the mood of the times than a steady and constantly powerful compulsion. It is this group, however, more than the 'educational and scientific estate' of Galbraith[1] that may really influence society by inaugurating new ideas and new movements. The 'estate' is, by definition, integrated into the inner-society. Dissent is more likely to come from the non-integrated students

[1] Galbraith, *The New Industrial State*, p. 288.

and affiliated intellectuals on the outside. As dissent fades and the pressures for social change become reduced within the inner-society, the students and their affiliated intellectuals become the main source of dissatisfaction and pressure for progressive change. This is a role of importance in any society.[1] It can be particularly effective when the change has merit and latent support from within the inner-society including from the 'educational and scientific estate' and even the 'techno-structure'. The new volatility of society based on instantaneous communication and lessened discipline of structured groups adds to the leverage of the dissenters when they have a cause with a strong moral base. Minorities can gain more attention more of the time. To be successful, however, their causes must be accepted and promoted by important elements within the inner-society; the dissenters outside require assistance from the initiators inside to be effective.

Capitalism created workers who changed capitalism. Modern industrialism creates students and intellectuals, whether seen as an 'estate' or an amorphous mass of the non-integrated or a combination of both, who in turn may help change modern industrialism. Their influence points in the direction of new evolutionary growth, not revolution—not revolution, in part, because, while some students and some intellectuals will always dissent, they are also always divided among themselves.[2]

A second outer-element is comprised of the elderly

[1] The effectiveness of a 'class' depends not only on the importance of its function, as Schumpeter has pointed out, but also how effective it is in performing its function. (Joseph A. Schumpeter, *Imperialism and Social Classes*, New York: Meridian Books, 1955.)

[2] The owners of education' tend to be more divided politically than the 'owners of property'. Property coalesces political attachments; education disperses them.

whose members are augmented by earlier retirement and longer life, and they now constitute ten per cent of the population of the United States. They too stand outside the inner-society with no clear sense of purpose in an economy that provides no creative use for the aged, and with a reduced level of income. They too may become concentrated in large numbers, as in the 'leisure worlds' of California and Florida where they live outside their family circle and away from the community of which they were once a part. Or they may coalesce into single-purpose political organizations, as under a MacLain in California or a Townsend nationally. Mostly, however, this outer-element is dispersed without any natural centre for activity such as the ghetto or the campus and is easily satisfied with better incomes and health care. It has no sense of unity with the other external elements of the under-class and the students and intellectuals—quite the contrary.

In the United States, the under-class and the outer-element of students have become associated to a degree in their interests against the government, the unions and the corporations. Both groups have in common an aspect of 'irresponsibility' since neither is playing a steady role in the economy and thus members of each are free of the compulsions and requirements and the discipline of jobs. They also constitute the main elements of inconsistency— and also islands of isolation—in a pluralistic society and, as Parsons has so often noted, societies seek consistency. This consistency has been largely achieved within the inner-society, but not with the outer-elements that constitute the new dualism. The ghetto and the campus come to be the remaining places where dissent is most keenly felt and most readily expressed. The university is placed in a particularly vulnerable position. As an institution it is affiliated with the inner-society, but many of its participants reject this affiliation and seek to use the institution as a base for dissent against the inner-society.

Thus society has moved a long way from the time when it appeared to Marx that the workers faced the capitalists in an irreconcilable conflict; or that class tensions would be ended when workers also became the gentlemen that Marshall wanted them to be. The new cleavages are not within the inner-society. They run according to a different logic than workers *versus* capitalists. The new cleavages come where the inner-society meets the under-class and the outer-elements. These are the locations of greatest friction. These cleavages are subject to being repaired—if repaired they can be—by other means than once proposed. The solutions are unlikely to be either the monolithic state or the perfect market.

# CHAPTER 9

# NEW "INHERENT CONTRADICTIONS"

1. All societies have 'inherent contradictions' and these contradictions may lead to change but not necessarily to dissolution. Pluralistic industrialism has its own set of contradictions.

A complex industrial system works best in harmony, yet finds itself with conflict endemic in it. Receding are the wars of city *versus* country, of workers *versus* capitalists. Taking their place are tensions over rewards and authority and conduct scattered at myriad points throughout the system. Group interests are fought out within the inner-society in some ceremonial battles but in many real ones too. In the United States, a new arena is opening up as public employees organize essentially against the taxpayers; and this conflict is harder to handle than that between workers and private employers. As we have seen, the under-class has become more active, and so also has the outer-element of the students. They wage conflicts over relationships with the inner-society.

New sources of tension are also opening up as the older democracy faces the new meritocracy based on technical skill—the 'expert-breakers' take the place of the older 'machine-breakers' and not alone in the China of Mao;[1] and as the 'modernists' and the 'traditionalists' face each

---

[1] Pen suggests that the antagonism towards the meritocracy can be reduced by a further equalization of incomes and encouragement of a plurality of values. (Pen, *Harmony and Conflict*, p. 245.)

other over the issue of constant change. The latter of these two conflicts turns 'Karl Marx upside down'. On issue after issue in the United States—equal access of all races to housing, environmental control, international relations—'the privileged have become the progenitors of change'.[1] The less privileged have become the conservatives not only on technological but also much other change. This is not so strange. The privileged generally have less to lose from change than the less privileged, have been better prepared to accept change, and see more need for it. Wall Street is more liberal and Main Street more conservative; big industrialists more progressive and workers more conservative. Change comes more from the top than the bottom of the inner-society.

Beyond all this lies the conflict over the appropriate limits for dissent in a society that becomes more interlocked, more fragile, more dependent on each person and each group cooperating effectively. Dissent is more of a problem because society becomes more volatile with better communications in total and with the intense pressure of television in particular. Lack of knowledge and apathy can no longer be counted upon to dampen dissent. The reaction time is quicker, the means of getting attention more readily available. The action of dissent and the reaction to it are both intensified. Thus the rules governing dissent and the treatment of it become much more crucial.

The answers, if answers there are to the contradiction of more conflict where more harmony is required, are dispersal of conflict over time and place, establishment of

[1] Louis Harris before the Foreign Policy Association, Washington, D.C., January 25, 1968.

116

reasonable rules of the game, and quick and effective settlement of disputes within the inner-society; and absorption of the under-class and reasonable adjustments to the demands of the students outside. These are tasks for the several managerial groups working together to keep the uneasy peace. Their tasks are made easier because economic progress yields the materialistic base for more and more concessions.[1] But a constant problem, as Madison knew it to be,[2] is how to handle the 'factions'; how to maintain balance among them.

2. A pluralistic industrial system, with many centres of power rather than none or one, is subject to exploitation. Some groups may build their Castles on the Rhine and take tribute from all who pass by. This has happened— in railways and public utilities and other monopolies, craft unions and medical associations. But society has by now had a good deal of experience with monopoly power, and has learned, where it has become excessive, to break it up or control it or escape it—more readily in product markets than in labour markets, but there too public pressures can have their impacts, as is now happening in the United States in the preparation of more doctors. The short-run costs of monopoly tend to be greater than the long-run. Beyond some point, as markets grow in size and as education spreads, the opportunities to create a really effective monopoly diminish; and 'competition among the few' becomes more effective.

[1] Pen describes how growth can contribute to the 'Great Harmony' in what he calls the 'confused society' of western capitalism where conflict does have 'positive significance' provided it is kept 'within bounds' as it has been. (Pen, *Harmony and Conflict*, Chapters 1, 2, 22, 23.)

[2] James Madison, Paper 'Number Ten' in *The Federalist*, New York: Modern Library, 1937.

## New 'Inherent Contradictions'

Stagnation in economic growth—or at least comparative stagnation—can and does occur in a pluralistic economy. There are solutions to stagnation, to a slow rise in productivity. One, as we have seen, is a heavy emphasis on institutionalized progress. A second is highly trained managers. A third is the elimination of class-conscious attitudes about work.[1] A fourth is bargaining structures which permit and even encourage bargains over benefits and over productivity at the same time—thus bargaining structures which are close to actual operations as in the United States. Yet there is an inherent conflict between progress and stability. All progress affects some one's stability unfavourably. The answer to institutionalized progress is institutionalized social security.

Inflation is another matter. The move to the 'labour standard'—as Hicks[2] called it—which reconciles full employment with the given wage structure, almost insures some inflation. Even aside from a generally inflationary situation, the wage system intends to inch its way up. Wages rise in one situation because of high profits, or a scarcity of a certain skill, or an aggressive trade union, and then this increase tends to spread into a smaller or larger or even very large surrounding area. As organization spreads and knowledge spreads, the area dominated by new patterns tends to spread also. Wages do need to be 'acceptable' as Hicks said and do constitute something of a system,[3] and so increases in one

[1] The longer they have existed, the harder they may be to eliminate. For a history of the early development of a working class consciousness in England, see E. P. Thompson, *The Making of the English Working Class*, London: Gollancz, 1963.

[2] *Op. cit.*

[3] More so in England than the United States. 'The outstanding characteristic of the national pay structure is the rigidity of its relationships.' (Guy Routh,

118

place, for whatever reason, do tend to encourage increases elsewhere where the original reason may not apply. This can become a particular problem in a period of excess demand when a major scramble starts to keep up with or get ahead of it. Those who get ahead may obtain only transient advantages, but these may be quite important to them at the time.[1]

The United States has found no full answers. Guide-lines[2] and wage stabilization work in the short-run and under favourable circumstances only. There are so many ways of evasion. The guideline, also, is more likely to become a floor than a ceiling; and the efforts to break the line can be most disconcerting politically—the line becomes a challenge rather than a control. Efforts at stabilization by government may even, at times, have inflationary results.[3] National voluntary agreements would appear to be more effective than imposed guide-lines; but national agreements make local productivity agreements less effective. An active labour market policy which seeks to reduce the initiating impulses, rather than control their extension once introduced, would seem to have more value under normal conditions. But this may be a problem for which there is no full solution;[4] nor may

*Occupation and Pay in Great Britain, 1906–1960*, Cambridge: University Press, 1965, p. 147.)

[1] Derek Robinson, 'Wage-Rate Differentials Over Time' *Bulletin* of the Oxford Institute of Statistics, November 1961.

[2] For a discussion of American experience see George P. Shultz and Robert Z. Aliber, *Guidelines, Informal Controls, and the Market Place*, Chicago: University of Chicago Press, 1966.

[3] Clark Kerr, 'Governmental Wage Restraints: Their Limits and Uses in a Mobilized Economy', *American Economic Review*, May 1952.

[4] 'So long as inflation continues, a centralised policy of wage stabilization is impossible; as soon as inflation ceases it will be unneccesary.' (C. W. Guillebaud, *Wage Determination and Wages Policy*, London: Nisbet, 1960, p. 19.)

it, within reasonable limits, really need one. Restraint is more asked for than granted; stability more sought after than achieved. Both restraint and stability may be too much to expect. The political leaders must seem to do something about inflation; the unions and business leaders in fact undo that something.

3. The individual faces the large organization. Organizations do have power over individuals but it is never absolute, and there is often surprising room for adjustments. Nevertheless, there are problems and they may grow as the labour force becomes more highly educated with higher expectations of personal freedom and responsibility. Two types of adjustments may be necessary.

First, jobs may need to be re-designed to create a sense of 'responsible autonomy.'[1] The job structure has an impact on education; but education also has an impact on jobs, and higher levels of education exert pressures job by job to broaden assignments, increase responsibility and introduce more autonomy from specific control.

Second, the internal market requires provisions to assure access on the basis of merit, a reasonable chance to participate in or influence the rule-making process, judicial protection from unjust penalties and expulsion, and freedom to withdraw without excessive costs in foregone rights including retirement benefits and medical provisions. Some of these rights may require guarantees by the state itself as against the power of the private governments. It may take the state to reduce the tyranny of the group; a strong state to protect individual autonomy. It is recognized that such individual rights can run

[1] Louis E. Davis, 'The Design of Jobs', *Industrial Relations*, October 1966.

counter to the stability of private governments and thus encourage these private governments—particularly unions—into external conflict as a result.

Outside the world of work—which of necessity requires considerable discipline and conformity—lies the world of private life which increasingly allows a variety of endeavour and conduct as an offset to the heavy demands for conformity of the world of work. This is particularly true in the large city of modern industrialism as against the one-industry town or rural area with its emphasis on conformity. A dual life becomes possible—one on the job, the other in leisure; the latter provides an avenue of escape from the inevitable discipline of the job. To the dual society with its under-class is added the dual life of the inner-society.

The pluralistic industrial society of today is rent with contradictions involving conflict and harmony, exploitation and constructive effort, control and individual freedom. Within this whole array of problems, it seems to me that the ones inherently most difficult of solution are integration of the under-class into the inner-society, adjustment to the dissent of the students and intellectuals, and control of inflation. These problems contrast with increasing working class conflict or permanent stagnation—the spectres raised by Marx and Marshall. Perhaps the main test will be whether new stability can be created as the old is constantly upset. The answer to this question separates the optimists from the pessimists.

# CHAPTER 10

# THE FUTURE OF PLURALISM

1. The old struggle was seen by Marx as being over the ownership of property since property determined power. The new struggle is directly over power, almost regardless of the ownership of property: power to set the rules, fix the rewards, influence the style of life. It takes place in modern industrial societies between the several forms of pluralism as against the monolithic society of Stalinism on the one extreme and anarchism without any central coercive authority at the other, and within and among the several forms of pluralism themselves. The old struggle pitted the workers under the banners of socialism against the capitalists with control of the state as the major prize. The new struggle pits the managed under the banners of freedom and participation against the managers with the control and the conduct of a myriad of organizations involved. Instead of trying to concentrate power in the state, the new effort is to fractionalize it everywhere—the old salvation is the new tyranny; and general revolution gives way to piece-meal evolution. Communism, not capitalism, now faces the greatest challenge, for power there is most centrally held—the old radicalism is the new conservatism. Communism out of power challenged capitalism in power, and the communists were the radicals; but now communism in power is challenged by the syndicalists out of power and the communists are the reactionaries. The gulf between the *status quo* and the new evolutionary

movement is now the greatest in communist-run societies. Less difficult is the challenge to the managerial pluralism of capitalism where the dispersion of the ownership of property has already led to a greater decentralization of power. But the challenge is still there.

Pluralism is the natural general form of modern industrialism but itself is subject to great variation in the roles given to the central authority, the organized group, and the individual. It is not just a 'domesticated version of the class struggle'[1] which was over property, but rather another chapter in the more eternal struggle over power. Syndicalism, not socialism and communism, constitutes the essential challenge to the *status quo* and particularly to the *status quo* of communism in the Soviet model. Syndicalism becomes a challenge as a result of better education, better communications, the removal of ancient restraints of belief and morality, better health and greater energy, as well as the inherent reaction against control and conformity. The battle is being joined. The more extreme alternative of anarchism is too irrational and too unworkable in a modern technological society, and the forces that really want it too weak for it to be a realistic possibility. Nor can syndicalism be successful in full; but it may find its historic destiny in partial solutions as has the socialist doctrine of working class supremacy. Anarchism is a natural tendency of some students and some intellectuals. Syndicalism is 'instinctive'[2] to workers as shown by the quick resort to works councils or Soviets or co-determination after a

[1] Robert Paul Wolff, 'Beyond Tolerance' in Robert Paul Wolff, Barrington Moore, Jr., and Herbert Marcuse, *A Critique of Pure Tolerance*, Boston: Beacon Press, 1965.

[2] Lichtheim, *Marxism in Modern France*, p. 198.

social earthquake. Syndicalism, and not only under such circumstances, is an essentially conservative as well as instinctive act—the desire to control what you have, to exercise the 'job control' (in the phrase of Selig Perlman) of a muted syndicalism as against the outside forces in society and the pressures of change. The coming struggle for power is over how far communism and capitalist pluralism may be drawn away from their coordinated and managerial forms towards syndicalism.

2. The traditional criticisms of pluralism are those noted earlier: that it cannot get harmony, avoid exploitation and provide freedom for the individual from group domination. New charges are now being advanced.

One charge is that pluralism stifles change, that it extends 'manipulation' from the hands of one central agency to the more effective hands of many groups; that 'containment of social change' is the 'most singular achievement of advanced industrial society.'[1] Change, particularly social change, is nearly always to a degree stifled. The amount of change, however, that can and does take place in the standard pluralism of capitalism is quite impressive—extension of democracy, acceptance of the trade unions and the welfare state, adoption of full employment policies and much else. Adjustments have been made to accept the causes of the students and demands of the ghetto residents in the United States in recent times. Rather than being closed to change, pluralism has been open to change, albeit somewhat sluggishly from the viewpoint of the reformers. Change is evolutionary and not by the dramatic dialectical process of opposite *versus* opposite that Marcuse favours.

[1] Marcuse, *Reason and Revolution*, pp. 22 and xii.

Powerful forces support change, or at least accept it. In fact, new technology, heavily subsidized, virtually forces some change. There are the dissenters—some students, some intellectuals, some representatives of the under-class. There are the initiators of change in the educational and scientific estate, the techno-structure, the top levels of industry, and progressive political circles. Together they generally overpower the no-change forces that now include some workers and many small business-men. It is the no-change group of the 'little man' in the United States that rather feels put upon by the more progressive leadership circles supporting reform through 'big government'. The more successful and more flexible face the less successful and less flexible. Pluralism, under its leaders, has not been a conspiracy against change.

A second charge is that pluralism, but not pluralism alone, allows the economic system to dominate life—to dominate leisure, culture, politics, education. Galbraith speaks of 'its monopoly of social purpose';[1] Marcuse of how 'the productive apparatus tends to become totalitarian to the extent to which it determines not only the socially needed occupations, skills, and attitudes, but also individual needs and aspirations.'[2] This charge could be made against all societies in history since economic activity has, of necessity, been a central concern. Greater wealth, better education and democratic processes each provide escapes from this domination, and pluralism permits and even supports each of them. As man moves farther away from economic necessity, he becomes more

[1] Galbraith, *The New Industrial State*, p. 399.
[2] *Op. cit.*, p. xv.

free to adopt multiple standards for success and conduct, and not just economic ones alone.

The third charge is that pluralism fosters group welfare and not the welfare of the total community—the general welfare.[1] This is true to the extent that pluralism approaches community welfare through group interests; and not all groups have equal power and influence. Given freedom of association, however, groups will form— including groups devoted to the general welfare—and will thus stand between the collectivity and the individual. How else it might be has not been made clear, unless some group with a monopoly on the 'truth' about group welfare were to be in full control. Short of such an authoritarian solution, the approach to the general welfare must be an aggregative one.

Pluralism does have these problems: containment of group conflict, avoidance of exploitation, protection of the individual from excessive group control, the effective handling of change, the proper influence of economic activity in the total life of society, and the reasonable achievement of the general welfare. Beyond these problems, it is hard to govern with so many highly organized and relatively autonomous groups, with divided loyalties, and with such lack of a clarity of 'principles' that unite as against interests that divide. None of these problems, however, has proved as fatal as class conflict and stagnation might have been. There is a basic harmony in western pluralism based on democratic processes, market mechanisms, full employment and growth. In the United States, the two most pressing problems are further equalization of opportunity and

[1] See Wolff, in *A Critique of Pure Tolerance*.

income to benefit the under-class, and further integration of isolated groups like some students and some intellectuals. Equalization of opportunity for other categories of individuals (as farmers) and integration of other groups (as workers) has been successfully undertaken in the past.

3. A basic contradiction will still exist, however, between the more highly educated and independent individual wishing more identity to his life as against the necessary existence of larger and larger organizations[1] and the inevitable development of potentially more dominant technology. The individual will be partly slave and partly free, but the proportions of each are important. There are a number of ways in which individual freedom can be increased within modern industrialism:

(1) Decentralization of large organizations.
(2) Diversification of endeavours among both independent units and units of large organizations.
(3) Provision of maximum freedom of choice to select among the diversified endeavours; which means, as an antecedent, full opportunity for an education commensurate with ability.
(4) Increased opportunities for participation within each unit; although everyone cannot be a manager.
(5) Protective rules that provide against undue control; and against improper discharge and limitations on freedom to leave (as with retirement plans that are not vested).
(6) Provision of the maximum number of options—

[1] Raymond Aron sees individuality *versus* collectivity as one of the ultimate contradictions; the others being equality *versus* hierarchy, and diversity *versus* universality. (*Progress and Disillusion*, New York; Prager, 1968.) Each of these contradictions is intensified by industrial society.

in hours of work, timing and length of vacations, retirement benefits, educational opportunities, even rates of pay—as against the rigidities and uniformities of the 'standard rate' approach.

(7) Design of jobs to enrich and enlarge them.

(8) Wide latitude for style of life off the job.

These possibilities, it may be noted parenthetically, can be applied almost equally to the campus as to the plant.

Alienation, as Freud noted, is one price of civilization, for civilization confines as well as frees individuals. Alienation, however, can be reduced by adjusting society to the individual, rather than only the individual to society. In this sense industrial society can be made more humane.

The 'free choice society'[1] of liberal pluralism could provide more of the 'inner freedom', the 'private space', that some now seek, and within the framework of pluralism. It could provide many small utopias with the likelihood that some will be closer to the definitions of disparate individuals than could the one big utopia which so many men have sought for so long with its conformity, its advance definition by others, its search for the one perfect organizing principle. This will require tolerance. These many utopias can only be approached gradually and by piece-meal reform, not through revolution. They will make more nearly possible multi-dimensional man in a fully multi-dimensional society. The human spirit will be more nearly liberated.

I suggest that the convergence within pluralism will be towards liberal pluralism. Trade unions and communist parties may come to be among the new conservatives in

---

[1] I am indebted to Gosta Rehn for this phrase in an unpublished manuscript.

the course of this convergence. They represent so often
in their ideologies and their practices what Michels called
'the iron law of oligarchy';[1] they stand for unity, for
disciplined action, for central control in the face of the
class enemy. The new problems of modern industrial
society call for more flexibility, for more individuality.
The new imperative is to 'humanize' the communities of
work, adapt them to individual preferences. Rather than
the unfolding of class relations or the perfecting of
market mechanisms, the new force at work is further
adaptation to individual preferences in many situations
and for many reasons. The challenge once was to absorb
and adjust to the factory, the worker and the capitalist;
now it is to adjust to the more aggressive individual.
Instead of socialism challenging the old capitalism, it is
now anarchistic and individualistic and syndicalistic
tendencies challenging the new communism and the new
capitalistic pluralism. A new synthesis is in process.

4. Marx stood for the collectivity reached through
class warfare; Marshall for the individual serviced by the
market. In the interim, industrial pluralism has developed
as the realistic alternative to both the monolithic and
the atomistic society. Pluralism now struggles with
some of the ultimate issues that go beyond class *versus*
class and monopoly *versus* the market: (1) the role of the
managed as against the managers, of the semi-managed
as against the semi-managers, of the individual against
the group; (2) the pressure of the ever newer technology to change the lives of men as against the desire
of men to rule technology, to exercise their options
in relation to it; (3) the interests of those inside the

[1] Robert Michels, *Political Parties*, New York: Free Press, 1966.

productive process as against those standing outside; and (4) the contrast between the imperfectibility of man and the hope for a more perfect society. No revolution, no alchemy of morality and knowledge can rid man of all his chains, can make all men into gentlemen; or so it seems one century later. We can only envy the optimism of Marx and Marshall that surrounded their views of the evolution of the working class.

# INDEX

affluence, increase of 28, 64; problems of 71, 75
agitation, as match to light fires of revolution (Marx) 36
agriculture, neglected by Marshall and Marx 69
alienation, as consequence of machines under capitalism (Marx) 21–2, 26, 35; in large-scale industrial societies 31; as one price of civilization 128; of students 111
anarchism 107, 122, 123
apprenticeship, trade unions and 46, 49, 52, 102
Arendt, Hannah 41, 42
artisans, as intermediate class (Marshall) 33
authority, under industrial pluralism 79, 80
automobile, as symbol of high mass-consumption 75

*Bee-Hive*, Marshall contributes to 8
Bell, Daniel 76
Bendix, R. 39
Bentham, Jeremy 2
Boulding, K. E. 76
bourgeoisie, and feudalism (Marx) 35; and proletariat (Marx) 36
bricklayers' unions, Marshall on 47
Brinton, Crane 41, 42
Britain, general strike in 38; main field of study for both Marshall and Marx 6, 15–16; Marshall on class consciousness in 34, 43; Marshall on 'stiffness' of capitalism in 19, 30; Marx on class structure of 42–3, 67

building workers, entry to trade of, in U.S.A. 52, 105
bureaucrats 71, 77; of business corporations 86; of trade unions 99
business corporations, as private governments 84–5; profit not now sole test for 71, 84

Cairnes, J. E. 57
Cambridge economics, Marshall's hopes for 13, 39
capital, accumulation of 25, 63; human or personal (Marshall) 30, 46, 65, 91; mutual dependence of labour and (Marshall) 34, 66; new investment of, in U.S.A., as percentage of G.N.P. 94
capitalism, 'cheerful stage' of 5; democracy and 68; guided 70; increasing misery under (Marx) 25, 26, 27, 35; opposing views of Marshall and Marx about future of 19–32, 62, 74
capitalists, as social class (Marx) 34–5; *see also* entrepreneurs
character, effect of work on 14, 93
China, revolution in 40, 41
Christian Socialists 2
citizens, workers as 37, 96
class collaboration, and class conflict 33–43, 62
class conflict, and class collaboration 33–43, 62; ideology of, now exhausted 89; incompatible with industrialism 96, 98; replaced by manipulation? 77; still an element of capitalism in 1930s 66

# Index

class consciousness, in ghettos 103; under industrial pluralism 96, 97; of manual workers in Britain (Marshall) 34, 43; about work 118

classes, social, Marshall on 33–4; Marx on 34–5, 63; merging of 37, 43, 63–4; new 71

classless society, aim of both Marshall and Marx 10–11, 17, 62, 70; aim of all practical leaders of all industrial societies 98

closed shop, 52

collective action, emphasized by Marx 3

Commons, J. R. 44, 74, 78

communications, and dissent 106, 116; and revolution (Marx) 36

communism, appeals to earlier stage of development than Marx foretold 40; modified to coordinated pluralism 79, 80; syndicalism as challenge to 122, 123

Communist Parties, Marx's hopes for 13, 35; as new conservatives 128–9

competition, monopolistic 68

compromise, willingness for 39, 43

compromise benefit (Marshall) 87

concentration of industry, observed by Marshall and Marx 14, 63, 65

conflict, of classes, *see* class conflict; methods of dealing with 116–17; now fractionalized and contained 37–8, 43, 72, 87, 90

consensus, basic, contribution of trade unions to 48; necessary in industrial society 83n, 97, 109

conservatives 78; new (less privileged classes) 116, (the old radicals) 123, (trade unions) 99, 128–9, (working class) 82

consistency, sought by societies 113

consumers 77

consumptionist society 75

cooperative movement 70; Marshall and 9, 45

coordinated pluralism 79, 80, 124

craft unions 49, 58, 101–2

craftsmen, labour market for 93, 102; restriction of output by 60

crises, industrial, as opportunities for revolution (Marx) 36, 40; of overproduction (Marx) 20; *see also* depressions

Cuba, revolution in 40, 42

'custom', in wage rates, 50, 52, 86

Dahrendorf, R. 75

Davies, James 41, 42

democracy, and capitalism 68; Marshall and 45, 65; Marx and 64; and meritocracy 115; revolutions caused by middle-class seeking 99

democratic processes, in industrial pluralism 126

depressions, expected by Marx to increase 20, 31, 63; money, wages in 20, 49, 52; not considered important by Marshall 20–1, 31, 65, 67; policy to counteract 39, 64, 66

dialectical materialism 66

dissent, conflict over appropriate limits for 116; ghettos as centres of 108, 114; universities as centres of 106–11

division of labour, *see* specialization

Dobb, Maurice 63

doctors, in U.S.A. 52, 117

economic forces, dominant in period of Marshall and Marx 69; industrial pluralism and 125; now share dominance with politics 71; trade unions should not go counter to (Marshall) 47; and wages 50

education, and access to inner-society 90, 94; and choice of trade 58; extension of 71, 90–2; as investment (Marshall) 29–30, 46, 65, 91; in period of Marshall and Marx 69; and political attachments 112n;

132

# Index

# Index

5, 69–70, 73; Marx seldom mentioned by 62; points of agreement between Marx and 6–18; predictions of 64–8; stood for: the free market 61, the individual serviced by the market 129, personal interest 2

Marx, Karl, better as saint than as prophet 42; disagreed with Marshall on future of capitalism 19–32, 62, 74; historical period of 5, 69–70, 73; Marshall never mentioned by 62; points of agreement between Marshall and 6–18; predictions of 62–4, 67–8; stood for: the authority of society 2, collectivity reached through class warfare 129, a social plan 61

Mayo, Elton 78

merit, in labour market 93, 120

meritocracy, antagonism towards 115

messianic quality, of Marshall and Marx 16, 17

middle class 37, 43, 99

migrant workers in U.S.A. 103

Mill, John Stuart 2, 45, 57, 62, 93

misery, increasing under capitalism (Marx) 25, 26, 27, 35; from psychological deprivation 107; of rising expectations 40, 72, 102–3

mobility, of labour 57–8; of leaders 87; social 97

monopolistic competition 68

monopoly, as alternative to free market (Marshall) 65; public pressures against 117

morality, collective (Marx) 74; higher individual, as means for social improvement (Marshall) 6, 11–12, 74; of inner-society and under-class 102; trade unions and (Marshall) 45–6, 47, 48, 56, 59; Victorian 69

mutual aid, worthy activity of trade unions (Marshall) 46

Myrdal, G. 100, 102

national income, share of labour in 15, 25, 31

nationalism 64, 71, 99

non-profit institutions, in U.S.A. 86, 95

offices, labour market for 93

old people, as outer-element of society 112–13

opportunity, equalization of 126–7

optimism, of Marshall and Marx 11–12, 17, 69, 130

organizational revolution 76

outer-elements of modern society 82, 90, 99; conflicts of, with inner-society 114, 115; old people as section of 112–13; students as section of 106–12, 117, 121

output, restrictions on 19, 46, 59–60

overtime 102

Owen, Robert 3

participation, desire for 71, 88, 90, 122; students and 107, 110

peasants, not important in revolution (Marx) 36, 64, 67; revolutions among 40, 99

perfectibility of man, *see* human nature

personal interest, doctrine of (Marshall) 2

piece rates 47, 48, 53

Pigou, A. C. 8, 84

pluralism, pluralistic industrialism, *see* industrial pluralism

political parties, with working-class support 38, 39, 70, 99

political struggle, class conflict as (Marx) 36

politics, economic forces and 67–8, 71; economic liberalism and 28

politicians 71

population, problems of increase of 71–2, 76; surplus, and wages (Marx) 27

135

# Index

post-bourgeois society 76
post-capitalist society 75
post-civilized society 76
post-industrial society 77
poverty, Marshall's concern with problem of 8
power, centres of 83, 84, 111; struggle for 122, 123, 124
predictions, by Marshall 64–7, and Marx 62–4; lessons from 67–8; power of 68
private governments 83; business corporations as 84–5; individual rights and 120–1; trade unions as 85–6
private life, variety in, as against conformity in work 121, 128
problems, do not necessarily get worse 68
production, increasingly interdependent processes of 82, 83
productivity 59, 60, 118
professional personnel 33, 71
profits, 14; high, and wages 52; not now sole test for business enterprises 71, 84; orientation of capitalists towards 69; tendency to declining rate of, seen by Marshall and Marx 15, 20, 28, 63
progress, institutionalization of 94, 95, 118; pressure for, from students and intellectuals 112
proletariat, stages of development of (Marx) 35; *see also* working class
property, class struggle over ownership of (Marx) 80, 122, 123; and political attachments 112n
public administrators 71
public employees, organize against taxpayers 115

quality of life 94

race, and class consciousness, in U.S.A. 103
race relations, working class and 98

radicalism 78, 80; Marx as high priest of 2, 70; the old, as new conservatism 123; of students 110; syndicalism as the new 80, 122, 123; *see also* socialism
rationality, individual and collective 74
religion 69
rentiers, as social class (Marshall) 33
restricted entry, to trades and professions 52
retirement benefit 120
revolution, capitalism expected to end in (Marx) 6, 19, 31, 36, 40, 70, 72; observed sources of 99; organizational 76; theories of causes of 41–2
Robinson, Joan 5, 63
Rostow, W. W. 75
Russia, revolution in 40, 42; student dissent in (Czarist) 106

Saint-Simon, Comte de 2
Samuelson, P. A. 28
Scandinavia, active labour-market policy in 104
Schumpeter, J. A. 3, 76, 110
scientists 71, 77
self-employed workers 34
seniority, in labour market 58, 93
service class, service trades, service workers 34, 71, 75, 85
Shove, G. F. 65
skills, effect of machines on, (Marshall) 23, 65, (Marx) 23–4; increase in 31, 95; reduction of wage differential for 50, 51
Slichter, S. A. 43, 74
Smith, Adam, 2, 45
social change, under industrial pluralism 124–5, 126
social security, institutionalized, as answer to institutionalized progress 118
socialism, Marshall and 9, 12, 16, 32, 65; Marx and 2, 11, 61; now

# Index

historically exhausted 70–1, 73
society, doctrine of authority of
  (Marx) 2, 3; multi-dimensional
  (industrial pluralism) 82–114
specialization (division of labour),
  consequent on use of machines 31;
  as viewed by Marshall 23; as
  viewed by Marx 21, 22, 63
stability, conflict between progress
  and 118
standard of living, seen by Marshall
  as rising 24–5
standard rate of wages 46, 51, 101,
  119
state, the, industrial pluralism and
  79; Marshall's and Marx's views
  of 15, 84; primitive 69; protection
  of individuals from groups by 120;
  views on present nature of 17,
  74–7; and wages 54; and welfare
  15, 39, 48; see also 'laboristic
  state', welfare state
status differentials, fine gradations of
  97; replace class relations 16, 37,
  72
Stigler, G. 65
strikes, 47 48n
students 71; conflicts of, with inner-
  society 115; as outer-element of
  society 106–12, 117, 121; and
  under-class 113
syndicalism 107, 123–4; as new radicalism 80, 122, 123

Tannenbaum, F. 78
Tantner, R., and M. Midlarsky 41
taxpayers, public employees organize
  against 115
technicians 71, 77
technology 13–14, 20, 68; effects of
  72, 76–7; forces social change 125,
  129; inner-society and 95; working
  class and 98
techno-structure 75, 112, 125
technotronic, future society as 76
television 116

Tito 70
Tocqueville, Alexis de 2, 78
trade unions 39, 70; and group
  interests 44–61; Marshall and 9,
  44–51, 65; Marx and 35, 38, 44;
  as new conservatives 99, 128–9;
  as private governments 85–6
'transition class' (Marx) 34–5

under-class 37, 82, 90, 99, 102–6;
  conflicts of, with inner-society
  114, 115; membership of, defined
  by rejection 100, 102; problem of
  absorption of, into inner-society
  117, 121, 127; students and 113;
  see also lumpen-proletariat, unemployables
under-developed and developing
  countries, appeal of communism
  to 40–1; likelihood of revolution in
  64; problems of 72
unemployables (Residuum), as social
  class (Marshall) 15, 33, 47, 65, 100,
  101
unemployment, expected by Marx
  to increase 20, 27, 101; mass,
  neglected by Marshall 21, 65, 66;
  and wages (Marx) 27
United States of America, background of slavery, not feudalism,
  in 81; industrial pluralism in 82–
  121
universities, as centres of dissent
  106–11, 114–15; under industrial
  pluralism 94–5, 114
Utilitarians 2
Utopians 2, 69
Utopias, many small rather than one
  large 128

Viner, Jacob 6, 12–13
violence, weapon of students 110; of
  under-class 103, 104

wage-drift 51, 53, 54

137